Learning to Listen, Learning to Teach

The Power of Dialogue in Educating Adults

Revised Edition

Jane Vella

JOSSEY-BASS
A Wiley Company
www.josseybass.com

Published by Jossey-Bass
A Wiley Imprint
989 Market Street, San Francisco, CA 94103-1741   www.josseybass.com

Jossey-Bass books and products are available through most bookstores. To contact Jossey-Bass directly call our Customer Care Department within the U.S. at 800-956-7739, outside the U.S. at 317-572-3986, or fax 317-572-4002.

Jossey-Bass also publishes its books in a variety of electronic formats. Some content that appears in print may not be available in electronic books.

Library of Congress Cataloging-in-Publication Data

Vella, Jane Kathryn, 1931–
   Learning to listen, learning to teach : the power of dialogue in educating adults / Jane Vella. — Rev. ed.
        p. cm. — (The Jossey-Bass higher and adult education series)
Includes bibliographical references (p.   ) and index.
   ISBN 0-7879-5967-7 (alk. paper)
   1. Adult learning.   2. Adult education.   3. Teaching.   I. Title.   II.
Series.
   LC5225.L42   V45   2002
   374—dc21
                                                    2002003807

Printed in the United States of America
FIRST EDITION
PB Printing   10 9 8 7

Contents

Part Three: Becoming an Effective Teacher of Adults

Foreword to the 1994 Edition

I feel obliged to open this foreword with a warning: You will enjoy reading this book so much that you may wonder whether you are learning anything from it. Let me assure you that you will learn more from it than from any textbook written by me (or anyone else). The deep lessons it contains creep up on you and flower into joyful insights.

Jane Vella is one of the most gifted adult educators I have known. She has discovered and mastered the fundamental concepts of adult learning and applies them with flair, imagination, and loving, tender care. But she is more than a gifted teacher—she is also a gifted storyteller. If you find it difficult to put a good novel down at lunchtime, you will find it hard to put this book down for the same reason; you will get caught up in her exciting adventures.

Although I have written eighteen books on the subject myself, I must admit that I was surprised at how much I learned about the theory and practice of adult education from this book. But I am also delighted and rewarded by how much I learned about the people and cultures of lands I have never visited—northern Ethiopia, Tanzania, Indonesia, the Maldives, Nepal, El Salvador, Zimbabwe, Bangladesh. I understand our world better now; I am a more competent global citizen. I have a cadre of new friends: Fatuma in Ethiopia, Auni Makame in Tanzania, Margie Ahnan in Java, Mustafa

Hussein in the Maldives, Durga Bahadur Shrestha in Nepal, Mikaeli Okolo in Zambia, Carlos Castillo in El Salvador, Tainie Mudondo in Zimbabwe, Assura Lori in Bangladesh. Jane Vella made them come alive to me.

Have one of the most enjoyable and rewarding trips of your life!

January 1994   Malcolm S. Knowles
                                         Professor Emeritus
                                         North Carolina State University

Preface to the Revised Edition 2002

Adult educators around the world have reported that the ideas and skills taught in this book present a new way of teaching. Some have told me they find it a new way of thinking about learning. Others have said it is a new way of thinking about life.

When I read Danah Zohar's *Rewiring the Corporate Brain* (1997) and found her celebrating the new science of quantum physics as a new way of thinking and acting, I immediately recognized a connection between *Learning to Listen, Learning to Teach* and what she was describing as quantum thinking. The word *quantum* defines a measure of energy. Quantum physics relates what has been discovered in the twentieth century about the universe as energy. Quantum thinking, as Zohar (1997) and Wheatley (1999) define it, takes that particular view of the universe into the social sciences. In this revised edition of *Learning to Listen, Learning to Teach* I have used selected quantum concepts to enhance the study of adult learning.

We are at a critical moment in history when sheer numbers and violent events are driving us to rethink current educational paradigms and practices in professional training, industrial training, and community education in universities, schools, and colleges. How can we teach multitudes on a human scale? How can we share information peacefully? How can we reach workers for retraining, senior citizens for varied educational pursuits, youth for the skills and inspiration they need, citizens for the examination of necessary

innovative political policies? How can we organize to share new research pouring from laboratories and libraries? What sure principles
can guide us in this vast national and global enterprise? Current
concerns about the quality of education around the world urge us
to examine the state of the art and the competence of the science
and to search for ways to improve the adult education process.

Those questions are even more compelling in these first critical
years of the new millennium than they were when this book was
written in 1994. That this book has been used to shape the thoughts
and behaviors of many young adult educators puts a new slant onto
those questions. Today we must ask, *How well have the principles and
practices learned here worked? Why are they working?* And, most significant, *what kind of society does the education supported by these principles evoke?*

In 1994 I boldly responded to the publisher's query: "Will this
book be used as a textbook?" "Oh, it would be a very enlightened
professor who decided to use this as a textbook." Well, we have
some very enlightened professors out there. They and their students
have written to me to say that this book was one of the keys un-
locking the discipline of adult education for them. This book is
being used by community educators throughout the world. It is used
currently by staff of Habitat for Humanity and Freedom from
Hunger, two development agencies working in communities around
the globe.

Scope of This Book

This is a book about teaching and learning. As a teacher of adults
for more than fifty years I have worked in the United States, Africa,
Asia, Latin America, Europe, and the Middle East. Through these
experiences of teaching I have gleaned some profound lessons about
learning. I share in this book some of these lessons through a series
of stories about teaching events around the world in which the
power of dialogue in the midst of diversity was effective.

What Is New

This revised edition is a great opportunity for me to share with you some of what I have learned since 1994. It provides a taste of the principles and practices in *Training Through Dialogue* (1996), the evaluation models in *How Do They Know They Know?* (1998), and the latest research on learning tasks in *Taking Learning to Task* (2000). You will discover a new theoretical perspective here as well, one gleaned from the discipline of quantum physics.

My dear friend, Michael Culliton, began talking to me about Margaret Wheatley and Danah Zohar and quantum theory years ago. Finally, he sent me two books, Wheatley's *Leadership and the New Science* (1999) and Zohar's *Rewiring the Corporate Brain* (1997). I realized as I read the books that the authors' research from the world of physics, psychology, and organizational behavior and my efforts in research on learning were closely related. This revised edition of *Learning to Listen, Learning to Teach* is designed from a base of what Wheatley and Zohar call quantum thinking. Zohar (1997) describes quantum thinking as new-paradigm thinking: holistic, integrated, spiritual, energetic. Classical physics, based on Isaac Newton's theories, is the basis of our traditional understanding of not only our physical universe but also of the social, economic, and political patterns that have emerged since the seventeenth century. Newton was himself bound by the dualistic nature (good-evil, true-false, matter-spirit) of his inherited philosophy. No one questions his contribution. Joseph Campbell tells the story of the response of a team of astronauts in one of the early space flights. When they were asked by Houston Mission Control, "Who is navigating now?" they replied, "Newton."

Classic Newtonian physics and quantum physics are both at work in our world. Newton's laws of motion set out a universe of constants, determined and separate from one another. Developments in quantum physics have offered a new perspective on the universe and our place in it. As I searched for comprehensible renditions of classic theory on the Internet, I found a page that laid out Newton's laws of motion clearly and concisely. I wrote a short e-mail note to the author, David Stern. He responded from his office at NASA, "What in the world could be the connection between quantum theory and education? Are you thinking of it as a metaphor?" I believe this engineer had probably never experienced dialogue education in which the process is deeply relational and quantum concepts are not metaphorical at all.

In a recent *New Directions for Adult and Continuing Education* publication, I describe a note I read as I stood in front of Rodin's sculpture "The Thinker" at an exhibit at the North Carolina Museum of Art. Rodin had written: "Notice that the thinker is thinking with his toes." *That* is quantum thinking. I understand such thinking as the kind of perception that recognizes the connection of all things and the vitality of natural energy. Again, Joseph Campbell offers this good advice from his research: "Live in accord with nature and nature will offer you her bounty" (Campbell, 1988). Learning can also be in accord with nature. This book invites new light on our epistemological research from a theory of natural philosophy. So prepare yourself for a quantum leap into a familiar place.

What Is Old

Since so many adult educators have found the stories and the principles in this book useful, I decided not to change these. Therefore, the format of the book remains the same. The twelve principles and practices are the same:

Needs assessment	Learning with ideas, feelings, and actions
Safety	Immediacy
Sound relationships	Clear roles and role development
Sequence of content and reinforcement	Teamwork

| Praxis—action with reflection | Engagement |
| Respect for learners as decision makers | Accountability |

The stories are renewed, rewritten, and shared from the perspective of quantum thinking. Dialogue features as the macro-principle central to all twelve principles and practices. However, my explanations and my views of the situations where they were used are different. Quantum thinking sees each separate unit as a part of the whole. This kind of thinking recognizes the importance of context: no decision is apolitical, no action is nonpartisan, no thought is untouched by our own experience and particular view of the world. Quantum thinking uses dialogue as its basic tool not only for communication, but also for understanding. Chapter Two looks more closely at the potential of quantum thinking for understanding these adult learning principles and practices.

Each event related here underscores one of the twelve principles or practices. At the beginning of each chapter in Part Two, I name and describe the principle being featured. The events of the story show the educational potential of that principle or practice. There are many other principles and practices to guide adult educators, of course. I have fifty more stories to tell. Some of those stories have been told in *Training Through Dialogue* (1996) and *Taking Learning to Task* (2000). On my Web site [www. janevella.com], I am experimenting with new ways to share the power of dialogue as I perceive it at work around the globe.

What Is Special

A significant issue when educating adults is the perceived distance between teacher and student: between doctor and patient, between lawyer and client, between social worker and troubled parents, between judge and accused, between professor and adult learner. Until this distance is closed, the dialogue limps. The twelve stories in this book demonstrate the efficacy of closing that distance—of searching for means of honest dialogue across cultures, genders, classes, and ages. All of the principles and practices are indeed means to close that gap and develop that dialogue. An adult educator's first task, then, is to discover what mature students need and want to learn. This revised edition is a renewed dialogue with readers about the power of dialogue in adult learning. What I have discovered is that the dialogue is where learning really can occur for both teacher and participants.

The principles in this book invite dialogue, not as an abstract "right way" but as a developing process. How often have I heard and seen educators use monologue to "teach" the advantages of Freire's dialogue approach. Learners in that context were experiencing a dominating process to teach them the danger of domination and the uses of dialogue. I saw that it taught them, in fact, how to be dominators. We sometimes find the same domination patterns in university and community college education, health education, and professional training. A domination approach in adult education makes dominators.

We need to make a loud and clear statement that learning to listen to learners and learning to design for dialogue is an important option if we are building a civil society that can distinguish domination from democracy. I trust this book will be one guide to a greater congruence between what we are teaching and how we are teaching.

Socrates Taken to Task

I have learned that dialogue is not, as Socrates described it, only between teacher and student but rather also among students. In the kind of dialogue designed with these principles and practices, the teacher discovers herself to be a learner among learners, learning with her adult colleagues even as she designs the learning and manages the course. Small groups of adult students create a healthy learning environment—safe, challenging, demanding dialogical learning. My colleagues and I discovered over the past seven years that our aim was not teacher-centered learning, nor was it learner-centered learning. It was learning-centered learning: pragmatic, focused, accountable, sure (Gravett 2001).

Intended Audience

This book is for all who are concerned about the current educational challenge. If you are an administrator or a professor, a social worker or a health educator, a community education specialist or a physician teaching in a medical school, an entrepreneur or a journalist, or even a NASA engineer, in some aspects of your job you are an adult educator. Trainers in industry, literacy workers, nurses doing patient education, hospital and hospice staff welcoming and training volunteers, Peace Corps or National Service trainers and trainees—all can use these principles to enhance the educational work that is an essential part of their jobs. Often our work is with people whose cultural symbols and values are different from our own. These principles and practices are designed to show how our concern about using symbols that speak to other cultures can enhance the potential of learning for teacher and student alike.

Potential of the Book

I am continually touched by the response of very different people to the first edition of this book. Men and women of all ages, in various trades and professions, from many countries around the world tell me that the principles and practices described here are not new to them. "I always knew what I read here. It was very good to have my intuition corroborated." That phrase has come to me over and over again. I realized that readers were excited to learn about learning and to have their best ideas and hopes echoed.

This is a very personal book about a selection of significant educational experiences that illustrate the power of dialogue. I believe that when these twelve principles and practices are honored, learners can respond immediately to the query, *How do you know you know?* by saying, *We just did it!* Long-term indicators can then be put in place to examine how steadily they are "doing it" in their lives and their work, and how they have reconstructed the theory and practice to fit their context. We can measure the learning that occurs in a session, the transfer of skills and knowledge into workplace or home, and the impact on an organization or community or society. The demand for testing and competency-based education can be met, not through more severe tests, but through designs of accountable learning.

Such accountability is demanded not only of learners but even more of teachers. Make no mistake, it is tough doing dialogue education. As a dialogue educator you will wear a number of hats: designer, teacher, listener, learner. You will work hard to teach less and make more room for learning. The fact that it takes at least three hours to prepare adequately for one hour of this kind of teaching tells you just how demanding this approach is. The reward is that during that preparation, you, too, are learning! You are preparing not only content, but also process. You must construct the theory and practice you are teaching, as learners will when they use your design.

How can this new edition of *Learning to Listen, Learning to Teach* help you learn to use these principles in your own adult education work? Remember that reading this book is only the beginning of the dialogue. Reading the description of these twelve principles and practices and these stories can be a first step toward practice. However, the only way surely to learn them is to use them and then examine the immediate and long-term results both for yourself and the adult learners you serve. You must question and critique what is taught here, as well. Such feedback will criticize and question, praise and acclaim, renew and redo this dialogue approach so that it continues to grow and develop.

Approach

The approach of this revised edition is both deductive and inductive. It is deductive as I explain the principles and practices and demonstrate how to use them; it is inductive as I tell the stories and invite your response to these same principles in practice. The events took place in twelve very different situations around the world—in Ethiopia and Nepal, Tanzania and El Salvador, at a graduate school in New York and a migrant labor camp in North Carolina. The cross-cultural nature of the events gives evidence of the usefulness of the principle being demonstrated, which transcends cultural differences. The simplicity of the principles and practices shows that they can be applied productively in educational enterprises anywhere.

In each story chapter I review the principle that is the focus, identify the situation and setting for the selected learning event, study the learners and their needs, analyze the educational program and process, and examine one key principle of learning and teaching. I then point out the immediate indicators for evaluation of the learning, as well as the long-range indicators set in place to examine transfer of skills and knowledge and impact: the implication of that learning for life and work. At the end of each chapter there is a challenge to you that invites you to use the principle in some way appropriate to your own situation.

For twenty-two years, as a Maryknoll Sister, I taught in East Africa: Tanzania, Kenya, Zambia. Then, as assistant professor of adult education at North Carolina State University, I taught in Peru and rural North Carolina. Later, as director of Jubilee Education Center, I taught in Haiti, Chile, Zimbabwe, Lesotho, Swaziland, Ghana, and in McGee's Crossroads, a hamlet in rural North Carolina where migrant Haitian workers strove valiantly to learn English. As director of training for Save the Children, I taught in El Salvador, Honduras, Sudan, Korea, Ethiopia, Indonesia, Timor, Guatemala, Ecuador, Cyprus, Jordan, Bangladesh, Sri Lanka, and the Maldives, as well as on the American Indian reservations of

Arizona and New Mexico. Through this rich, international experience I have been able to name many principles for effective adult learning—principles recognized as effective in the fields of Ethiopia during the drought, on the islands of the Maldives, on the back porch of a migrant camp in North Carolina, in the villages of Tanzania. While these twelve principles and practices are familiar, my own particular interpretation of each one and the unique applications demonstrated in the stories are a function of my own personal experience and reflection.

To do this educational work, I rely on the work of many educators who are my teachers. They include Paulo Freire of Brazil, Humberto Maturana of Chile, Julius Nyerere of Tanzania, Malcolm Knowles, Alan Knox, and Carl Rogers of the United States, Kurt Lewin of Germany and the United States, and Carl Jung of Switzerland. To understand this dialogue approach in terms of quantum theory, I now can add new teachers: Albert Einstein, Erwin Schrödinger, and David Bohm. Danah Zohar and Margaret Wheatley, who interpret and apply quantum theory to social issues, are contemporaries. These researchers and scholars taught me from their books; the thousands of men and women I have met around the world taught me from their lives.

Overview of the Contents

In 1994 I did not have words for the kind of connections I perceived between all the stories and all the principles. In 1994, I was a good Newtonian scientist: noticing cause and effect, sure of a sound hypothesis, holding a rather static concept of reality. These twelve principles were to be the cause of enhanced learning!

However, there was an inherent contradiction between what I taught and Newtonian philosophy. I knew and taught that concepts were indeed re-created in the learning, that the learning environment was an operative context, not a merely cosmetic one. I recognized that my perception of the learners was at work in their learning, as was their perception of me and of the usefulness and immediacy of the content that they had to construct. This revised edition recognizes not only the phenomenon of these principles and practices at work but also the natural and physical theory that makes it all happen.

Part One comprises three chapters. Chapter One examines twelve principles and practices that ensure dialogue and effective learning. Chapter Two reviews six principles from quantum thinking as they relate to the twelve principles and practices. Chapter Three shows how these twelve principles and practices can be applied to ensure the effectiveness of an adult learning event. The next twelve chapters, Part Two of the book, offer specific applications of the principles and practices by describing twelve actual events. Chapter Four takes place in Ethiopia during a time of extreme famine and drought in the mountains north of Addis Ababa. Fatuma, the heroine of our tale, helps us realize how important it is to do a comprehensive needs and learning resources assessment before beginning a program. The implementation of this practice is the heart of that story and actually made the program work. Chapter Five tells of a development project in Tanzania near Lake Victoria, where the principle of safety was not used wisely enough to include an outsider. This example reinforces the need for safety for both adult learners and their teachers. Chapter Six describes how the relationship between teacher and learner informed and enhanced a one-on-one adult learning situation with an Indonesian physician, a Jubilee Fellow, working closely with fellow educators to learn the rudiments of dialogue education. This chapter demonstrates the cultural implications of such a learning relationship.

Chapter Seven takes place in rural North Carolina at a migrant labor camp where I taught English as a second language for a summer. It teaches the principles of sequence and reinforcement, showing how they enabled the Haitian migrant workers to grasp a great deal more than language skills. Chapter Eight tells of a long training course with development workers in the Maldives, an island nation in the Indian Ocean. The principle taught here is praxis: doing what you are learning. The anecdotes in this story demonstrate the value of praxis and show a variety of practices that implement the principle. Chapter Nine describes an adult education event in the Himalayan mountains of Nepal, demonstrating how learners develop when they are sure of themselves as subjects or decision makers in their own learning. Chapter Ten shows how adult learning can be made effective through the use of multilevel approaches (cognitive, affective, and psychomotor—ideas, feelings, and actions) in the learning task. The story takes place in a church community in Zambia. The adult learners were deeply moved and showed how much they had learned because we used this principle in the design of the program. Chapter Eleven takes place in El Salvador, where the principle of immediacy is manifest in all aspects of the event. It was a critical time in the history of the community development program and, indeed, of the country. Immediacy made for effective learning by all involved. Chapter Twelve moves to a graduate school in New York where the principle of role and role development helped professors adopt a new way of teaching. This group of learners, graduate school professors, was a long way from the islands of the Maldives or the Himalayan mountains. Even so, the same principles worked with them.

Chapter Thirteen moves back to Africa—to Zimbabwe immediately after independence—where we see how the principle and practice of teamwork enabled soldiers of the former army of liberation to transform themselves into literacy teachers for the new nation. They could not have learned what they learned in the short time available without working efficiently in teams. Chapter Fourteen takes place in eastern North Carolina, where we see the importance of engagement for the learning and development of critical thinking in a Hospice community. The final story, Chapter Fifteen, takes us to an international hospital in Bangladesh where the principle of accountability enabled doctors to learn a new way of teaching.

Part Three of this revised edition concludes the book. Chapter Sixteen, a summary and synthesis, offers further examples of how the twelve principles and practices can work for you. Chapter Seventeen, which shows how this book can make a difference in planning, teaching, and evaluating community and adult education, lists resources for further study. The appendix offers a set of suggestions on ways of doing effective needs and learning resources assessment.

The reader is invited to take part in each of these stories through the design challenge at the end of each chapter, where the key principle is presented as a possibility for application in your own educational work. A comprehensive reference section of materials relevant to dialogue education completes the book.

Acknowledgments

This revised edition is the gift to you all from Gale Erlandson and David Brightman, my editors at Jossey-Bass. The response to the first edition was so warm that they suggested doing an update, little knowing that it would be prepared by a "new" woman and from the perspective of the new science. So does synchronicity work! My collaboration with colleagues in South Africa, especially Sarah Gravett, has been important to this work.

Jossey-Bass invited three competent adult educators to review the first draft. Much of what you will find most useful in this new edition can be ascribed to their suggestions and advice.

Let me share Danah Zohar's cogent words: "Most transformation programs satisfy themselves with shifting the same old furniture about in the same old room. But real transformation requires that we redesign the room itself. Perhaps even blow up the old room. It requires that we change the thinking behind our thinking" (Zohar, 1997, p. 243). These critical times give added weight to her audacious challenge.

March 2002   Jane Vella
Raleigh, North Carolina

*This book is dedicated with affection
to the memory of my two teachers
Fay Honey Knopp and Lois Harvey
who taught me how to listen and,
therefore, how to teach.*

The Author

Jane Vella is the founder of Global Learning Partners, Inc., a company whose goal is to enable adult educators around the world to design and use dialogue in their education programs. Please see [www.globalearning.com] and [www.janevella.com] for more on the work of this company.

Vella received her B.Ed. degree (1955) from Rogers College in New York, her M.A. from Fordham University in 1965, and her Ed.D. (1978) from the University of Massachusetts at Amherst. Vella taught her first class in a third grade in Harlem in 1953 and has worked in community education in Africa, Asia, North and South America, the Middle East, and Europe since 1955. She has designed and led community education and staff development programs in more than forty countries around the world. She is the author of three other Jossey Bass books: *Training Through Dialogue* (1995), *How Do They Know They Know* (1998) (with Jim Burrow and Paula Berardinelli), and *Taking Learning to Task* (2000). Vella is now retired in Raleigh, North Carolina, where she plays piano, kayaks on a quiet lake, and continues her research on adult learning.

Part I

A Process That Works and Why

1

Twelve Principles for Effective Adult Learning

A principle, philosophers tell us, is the beginning of an action. As I begin the action of designing a course, a seminar, or a workshop for adult learners, I can make informed decisions that will work for these learners by referring to certain educational principles. I have discovered that these principles apply across cultures. In this first chapter of the new edition, we will examine twelve basic principles that are deeply interconnected, intrinsically related one to the other. In *Training Through Dialogue* (Vella, 1995) I name fifty such principles and practices that work to make dialogue education effective.

Although these principles and practices have been tested in community education settings, I believe they can also offer insight into educational processes for teachers and professors in more formal systems of education. As we shall see in the case studies that follow, they have been proven to work under diverse and sometimes extraordinarily difficult conditions.

One basic assumption in all this is that adult learning is best achieved in dialogue. *Dia* means "between," *logos* means "word." Hence, *dia* + *logue* = "the word between us." The approach to adult learning based on these principles holds that adults have enough life experience to be in dialogue with any teacher about any subject and will learn new knowledge, attitudes, or skills best in relation to that life experience (Knowles, 1970). Danah Zohar calls dialogue a quantum process, the means of doing quantum thinking (Zohar, 1997, p.136). In this approach to adult learning all twelve principles and practices are ways to begin, maintain, and nurture the dialogue:

- *Needs assessment:* participation of the learners in naming what is to be learned.

- *Safety* in the environment and the process. We create a context for learning. That context can be made safe.

- *Sound relationships* between teacher and learner and among learners

- *Sequence* of content and *reinforcement.*

- *Praxis:* action with reflection or learning by doing.

- *Respect for learners as decision makers.*

- *Ideas, feelings, and actions:* cognitive, affective, and psychomotor aspects of learning.

- *Immediacy* of the learning.

- *Clear roles and role development.*

- *Teamwork* and use of small groups.

- *Engagement* of the learners in what they are learning.

- *Accountability:* how do they know they know?

In my study of the new science, I have come to understand that my awareness of how interconnected these educational principles and practices are was sound quantum thinking. You will discover as you work with these twelve principles that you cannot exclude any of them.

What strikes me as significant and operative, as we begin to design for effective learning, is the distinction between the universe seen as a machine (Newton) and that seen via quantum physics as energy. It is the difference for me between materialism and spirituality, between rote learning and "thinking with one's toes." My experience of teaching and learning over my life of seventy years corroborates the quantum approach.

Principle 1: Needs Assessment

Doing an adequate needs assessment is both standard practice and a basic principle of adult learning, which honors the fact that while people may register for the same program they all come with different experience and expectations. No two people perceive the world in the same way. That's a standard axiom of quantum thinking. How can we discover what the group really needs to learn, what they already know, what aspects of the course that we have designed really fit their situations? Listening to learners' wants and needs helps shape a program that has immediate usefulness to adults. The dialogue begins long before the course starts.

Thomas Hutchinson (1978) of the University of Massachusetts, Amherst, offers a useful question for needs assessment: Who needs what as defined by whom? This WWW question—*who* as needers, *what* as needs, *whom* as definers—reveals the political issues involved in preparing a course for adult learners. Who are, indeed, the decision makers of this course? Is it the teacher? Is it the learners?

The answer, using quantum thinking, allows for both voices to be heard: adult learners must take responsibility to explain their context; the teacher must take responsibility to contact learners in every way possible, see them at work if possible, and be clear about what she can offer them. I cannot teach what I do not know. I have the issues and knowledge sets that I want to teach them. Adult learners, however, can name what they see needs to be taught, as well. They will vote with their feet if the course does not meet their needs. They will simply walk out. As their teacher, I need to discover what they already know and what they think they need or want to know. How do I hold these opposites, listen to these learners and their managers or their clients and to my own agenda, and then design a course that meets their needs?

This listening effort is what we call a learning needs and resources assessment. It is both a practice and a principle of adult learning. Paulo Freire (1972) refers to it as thematic analysis, a way of listening to the themes of a group. Themes are issues that are vital to people. When adult learners are bored or indifferent, it means their themes have been neglected in the design of the course. Motivation is magically enhanced, however, when we teach them about their own themes. People are naturally excited to learn anything that helps them understand their own themes, their own lives.

Myles Horton, founder of the Highlander School in Tennessee, discovered how well the police in that state understood this principle in the 1930s. As a young man he was arrested and indicted for "having gone to the miners, listened to them and then having gone back and taught them what you heard" (Adams, 1975, p. 33). In fact Horton was indicted for having done a needs assessment. "Listening to them" is the operative phrase here. How do we listen to adult learners, before we design a course for them, so that their themes are heard and respected? Today, we can use e-mail, faxes, and telephone conversations, we can use a small focus group to review the plan of a course or workshop or training, or we can do a survey. A well-distributed sample of even 10 percent of the group can give you important information for your design. The appendix offers numerous suggestions for ways of doing needs assessment.

Wheatley speaks of the advantage to dialogue and needs assessment of actually seeing people at work. "However you do it, discovering what is meaningful to a person, group or organization is your first essential task" (1999, p.149). Their themes are then visible and tangible. We can hear such themes by inviting them to describe situations they face, by asking for critical incidents in their work, by having a potluck supper where we can meet students with their spouses and partners in a relaxed atmosphere. I have used such events prior to each graduate course I taught at the School of Public Health at University of North Carolina in Chapel Hill. It is always a revelation for me to discover the surprising and exciting background of graduate students. I also spend five minutes on the phone with each student, calling each one from the list of those registered for the course. I discover things in such phone calls that help inform the course design. Remember that needs assessment does not form the course; it informs it. It is my duty as professor to determine what can be learned in the given time frame of a course; it is also my duty to begin the learning dialogue before the course begins.

My colleague, Dr. Paula Berardinelli, who was doing training in time management skills with a group of secretaries at a major industry, sent a number of them the draft program for the training a month before the event. She indicated that she would be calling them for a ten-minute conversation on a specified day. When she spoke with them, one by one, she heard a similar set of themes about their work. She also heard, over and over, how delighted they were by her call. They cited many incidents she could use in the training, as stories for analysis or case study material for reflection. This helped her understand some of the unspoken variables the secretaries faced. The result was a course that was accountable to the industry and to the adult learners, who knew they were decision makers in a sound relationship with the teacher. Although she spoke with only one-tenth of the group, the entire unit had heard of her needs assessment and were prepared at the outset of the course to offer their ideas spontaneously and creatively. All the secretaries said this had never happened to them before.

Using quantum theory, we see other alternatives for such a listening task: she might have gone to the company lunchroom and sat with the secretaries for a few hours of sandwiches and coffee. She might have asked to be a "fly on the wall" near the desk of one secretary for a day. I expect she would have gotten a clear sense of their learning needs in less than eight hours of observing. The case I cite in Chapter Four from the horrors of the drought-swept Ethiopian mountains is an extreme example of the need for a needs assessment. I cannot imagine what might have occurred there with those young teachers and Fatuma if I had not used Hutchinson's WWW principle: who needs what as defined by whom.

Principle 2: Safety

Safety is a principle linked to respect for learners as decision makers of their own learning. But it has an added connotation. It means that the design of learning tasks, the atmosphere in the room, and the very design of small groups and materials convey to the adult learners that this experience will work for them. The context is safe.

Safety does not obviate the natural challenge of learning new concepts, skills, or attitudes. Safety does not take away any of the hard work involved in learning. Should learning be designed to be challenging or to be safe? The answer is yes! Carl Jung, Swiss psychiatrist and teacher, suggests a pattern for addressing such dilemmas: hold the opposites! In the new science the question arises: Is light a wave or a particle? The only response is yes! It is seen as either a wave or a particle depending on the context, the state of the observer, and the kind of equipment used.

I suggest that in all our efforts, and certainly in regard to the presence of challenge and safety in our educational designs, we celebrate the opposites. Safety is a principle that guides the teacher's hand throughout the planning, during the learning needs and resources assessment, in the first moments of the course. The principle of safety enables the teacher to create an inviting setting for adult learners. People have shown that they are not only willing but also ready and eager to learn when they feel safe in the learning environment. What creates this feeling of safety?

First, trust in the competence of the design and the teacher enables the learners to feel safe. It is important to make your experience and competence clear—either through written materials that learners have read beforehand or through introductory words with them. This is a natural way to make learners feel safe and confident in their teacher.

Second, trust in the feasibility and relevance of the objectives makes learners feel safe. It is important not only to review the design with the group but also to point out how the objectives have been informed by the learning needs and resources assessment. You can point out that the objectives are empirically based, since they have been successfully used in similar sessions, and explain that you understand that this particular group is a unique context for this content to be learned. You will see physical manifestations of a feeling of safety appear after such a review of the whole design: people relax, smile, talk more freely to one another.

Third, allowing small groups to find their voices enhances the power of safety. One of the first learning tasks I do in any course is to invite learners to work in small groups to name their own expectations, hopes, or fears about a learning event or norms they want to see established in the large group. Four learners at a table large enough for their materials, small enough for them to feel included, provides physical and social safety for learners. You can hear the difference in the sound in the room as learners find their voices in the small group. The new science has demonstrated how context affects reality. I have seen how a safe context changes timid adult learners into assertive and daring colleagues. Using the principle of safety creates a context in which adults can do the hard work that learning demands.

Fourth, trust in the sequence of activities builds safety. Beginning with simple, clear, and relatively easy tasks before advancing to more complex and more difficult ones can give learners a sense of safety so they can take on the harder tasks with assurance. Sequence and reinforcement will be seen later as a corollary principle to safety.

Fifth, realization that the environment is nonjudgmental assures safety. Affirmation of every offering from every learner, as well as lavish affirmation of efforts and products of learning tasks, can create a sense of safety that invites creativity and spontaneity in dealing with new concepts, skills, and attitudes. Affirming is one of the basic tasks of every teacher. As we affirm what we hear, we invite learners to use the power they were born with as decision makers of their own lives. Teachers do not empower adult learners; they encourage the use of the power that learners were born with.

How can safety be endangered? One great danger to safety is the fatal moment when an adult learner says something in a group, only to have the words hit the floor with a resounding "plop," without affirmation, without even recognition that she has spoken, with the teacher proceeding as if nothing had been said. This is a sure way to destroy safety in the classroom. A "plop" destroys safety not only for the person who spoke, but for all in the room. Just as you can see physical manifestations as learners feel safer and safer, you can observe definite physical manifestations of fear and anxiety after such a "plop." You can watch the energy draining out of learners. The rise and fall of learners' energy is an accurate indicator of their sense of safety. Energy is another of our selected quantum concepts.

In the situation in Tanzania (Chapter Five), we see how safety was desperately needed to keep a gifted Muslim teacher working with a Christian community. We see how the absence of safety destroyed the potential of teacher and learners alike. How I wish I had known quantum theory and these principles at that time!

Principle 3: Sound Relationships

Sound relationships for learning involve respect, safety, open communication, listening, and humility. Zohar (1997, p. 134) offers a new reading of dialogue, *dia + logos*, as *dia* "through" and *logos* "relationship": "through relationship." She teaches that such dialogue is a central tool in quantum thinking.

The initial meeting between teacher and learner has to demonstrate the sense of inquiry and curiosity felt by the teacher. When doing a learning needs and resources assessment, through use of either e-mail, focus groups, or telephone surveys or by being a participant-observer in their work, we as teachers can discover specific personal or group learning needs. Then a dialogue about learners' expectations is a way to confirm our perception of their needs or amend it. Again, learners are immediately in the position of decision makers, deciding what they want to tell us, feeling safe enough to share their true feelings.

A manager of a nonprofit organization in Boston, about to attend a seminar at Tufts University, responded to a telephone call inviting him to name his unique learning needs for an upcoming management seminar by saying, "I am honored by this call. It's the first time anyone ever asked me what I wanted or needed to learn!" Imagine the relationship that was established between him and the professor via that simple phone call.

The power relationship that often exists between learner and "professor" can be a function of a mechanistic system where power is frequently used to dominate. Our efforts through dialogue education to build a world of equity and mutual responsibility cannot be designed without attention to the power of sound relationships. If I show how accessible I am to learners through an early dialogue in the learning needs and resources assessment, and respond to their questions with respect and affirmation in a safe environment, that world of equity already exists. We do "make the road by walking" (Freire and Horton, 1990).

In order to be sound, this relationship must transcend personal likes and dislikes and obvious differences in wealth and power. In such instances, a teacher knows she must be even more careful about showing respect, affirming, and listening carefully. When the teacher fails to show respect or fails to affirm a learner in a group or allows the fatal "plop," the whole group begins to doubt the learning relationship and often manifests anger, fear, and disappointment.

Nothing can diminish the importance to learning of the relation-ship between teacher and learner. The example in Chapter Six of Dr. Margie Ahnan from Indonesia shows how powerful a sound re-lationship can be in getting an adult learner to stretch beyond him-self and grow in the knowledge, skills, and attitudes he needs.

Principle 4: Sequence and Reinforcement

Sequence and reinforcement are vital but often overlooked as prin-ciples of adult learning. I have an axiom: do it 1,142 times and you will have learned it! Those 1,142 times should be properly se-quenced: from easy to difficult, from simple to complex. This seems such a basic concept. Failing to honor it, however, can lead to adults dropping out of courses, people acting out anger, fear, and disappointment, adults believing they cannot learn. As a budding pianist, I can corroborate that number, which in my case is im-mensely conservative.

Suppose a group of adult learners comes together to study opera. They are newcomers to the art. A focus group with three of them has shown that the learners want to know something of the devel-opment of the genre, but above all they want to learn how to listen to an opera for maximum enjoyment and intelligent response. The design ensures sequence and adequate reinforcement by taking a fa-miliar opera such as Puccini's *Madama Butterfly* and listening for five or six basic forms. The learning tasks would move from basic recog-nition of forms—That's an aria! That's recitativo!—to a judgment on the quality of the music, with use of new terms heard in demon-strations by the teacher. The teacher listens to the adult learners and then changes learning tasks to meet their needs for reinforce-ment. If the task is too difficult for most of the learners, it must be changed. This process is what we mean by learning as dialogue. It puts the adult learners in the position of decision makers as to what tasks are appropriate—in a healthy relationship with the teacher, who is not afraid to ask: How does this task feel at this moment?

Sequence means the programming of knowledge, skills, and attitudes in an order that goes from simple to complex and from group-supported to solo efforts. Learning tasks can be readily examined for sequence. Manifestations of safety and enthusiasm and readiness to achieve in learners indicate that sequence is being honored. When you, as teacher, see fear, confusion, and reluctance to try in the learner, test the sequence of the learning task. You may find you have not honored their need for small steps between tasks and their need for reinforcement.

Reinforcement means the repetition of facts, skills, and attitudes in diverse, engaging, and interesting ways until they are learned. The design of reinforcement in adult learning is the job of the teacher. Although adults may do their own reinforcement through practical work and study, our teaching designs, if they are to be accountable, must carry adequate reinforcement within them to ensure learning. This is the heart of the matter. In adult learning situations—in industry, community, family, or in learning sessions for personal advancement—the teacher is accountable for a design that works for the learners there and then. In formal school situations, young students are "taught" and then admonished to go home and learn what they have been taught so they can pass the test at the end of the course. They are accountable to the teacher. In adult learning, accountability is mutual. Busy managers attending a course on strategic planning, busy community people trying to learn how to organize for new legislation, families trying to learn how to communicate more effectively, individuals learning how to use a new word processing program—all need an accountable design and an accountable teacher providing the necessary tasks. Learners will do the work that enables them ultimately to know that they know. It is our job as designers of adult learning and teachers of adults to ensure that the principles of sequence and adequate reinforcement are honored within the learning program.

When we work diligently to design learning tasks that are in simple and sound sequence and that reinforce learning, we address the disparity in political power more directly than if we preach loudly on social and economic injustice. These rather technical principles and practices—reinforcement and sequence—are tough to use. They demand attention and diligence in design. When you do that hard work, you are in fact addressing sociopolitical-economic inequities. It is all of a piece. This is essential quantum thinking: the whole is more than the sum of its parts.

The example of building sequence and adequate reinforcement into a program preparing teachers to teach English as a second language and literacy skills to migrant workers in North Carolina (Chapter Seven) demonstrates the importance of this principle.

Principle 5: Praxis

Praxis is a Greek word that means "action with reflection." There is little doubt among educators that doing is the way adults learn anything: concepts, skills, or attitudes. Praxis is doing with built-in reflection. It is a beautiful dance of inductive and deductive forms of learning. As we know, inductive learning proceeds from the particular to the general, whereas deductive learning moves from a general principle to the particular situation. Praxis can be used in teaching knowledge, skills, and attitudes as learners do something with the new knowledge, practice the new skills and attitudes, and then reflect on what they have just done.

Learning tasks (Vella, 2000) are not practice but praxis. If inductive, they invite reflection or action on particular instances by using new content. If deductive, they consider new content and work to apply it in new situations. In each case, praxis demands a hard look at content, the re-creation of it to fit a new context, and essentially the testing of it to prove its usefulness. Again, quantum thinking helps us fathom how each learner has to re-create the content through participation. They redesign the skills, knowledge, attitudes they are learning as they see them fit their context.

Praxis is an ongoing process, of course. We use it in our daily lives all the time as we do something, reflect on its implications, and change. In a learning situation, we can use case studies inviting description, analysis, application, and implementation of new learning—that is, praxis. When we set a group of adults to practicing a skill and invite them, as subjects, to analyze the quality of their practice, that moves practice to praxis.

Zohar (1997, p. 148) shows that the questions we ask determine the kinds of responses we get. Such learning tasks give people the chance to practice new ideas, skills, or attitudes and immediately to reflect on them, thus making practice praxis.

The story of Mustafa Hussein and his community development colleagues (Chapter Eight) in the program in the Maldives offers specific examples of praxis. Their learning was a result not only of their action in the villages but also of quiet and reflection after that action.

Principle 6: Respect for Learners as Decision Makers

Respecting learners as decision makers of their own learning is a principle that involves the recognition that adults are in fact decision makers in a large part of their lives. Healthy adults desire to be subjects or decision makers and resist being treated as objects, something that can be used by someone else. In dialogue education, we assume that people are not designed to be used by others. Adults need to understand that they themselves decide what occurs for them in the learning event. The dialogue of learning is between two adults: teacher and student, learner and learner. For example, new content in a course can be shown to the learners with the question: What else do you feel you need to learn about this topic? This approach makes the content an open system inviting critical analysis, editing, and additions by adult learners. Quantum thinking goes beyond the subject-object dichotomy to recognize that inclusive respect honors all people as subjects in a universe of subject entities. As subjects, we evoke the world we perceive.

Here are some examples of ways to show learners they are respected as decision makers. When teaching something such as the facts of national history, we can always offer an open question that provides the vital element of choice: "Here are the dates of important events in the history of this nation. Which one seems the most important to you in terms of reaching independence? Why did you choose that date?" Before teaching the steps in a new computer program, the teacher can ask: "Which of these steps seems like it is going to be most useful to you in your work?" This question invites both teacher and learners to approach the learning as subjects. In teaching adults the personnel processes of a corporation in a job-related orientation program, the instructor can begin by asking an open question: "Here is our company process for taking sick leave. Look at all the steps. Which ones would be difficult for you? How does this process differ from the process you knew in another organization you worked for?"

In approaching adult learners as subjects, the teacher must distinguish between their suggestions and their decisions. This is called the distinction between a consultative voice (a suggestion) and a deliberative voice (a decision). Engaging adults in their own learning means engaging them as subjects of that learning. At times they offer suggestions; at times they make decisions. It is essential that we be clear about the difference.

Being perceived as the subject of one's own learning is powerful motivation to learning creatively. How can we offer adult learners as many opportunities for choice as possible? One practical guide is this. Don't ever do what the learner can do; don't ever decide what the learner can decide. As we shall see when we examine the principle of engagement, the learning is in the doing and the deciding. Teachers must be careful not to steal that learning opportunity from the adult learner. The example in Nepal (Chapter Nine) points out how one man's feeling himself the subject of his learning enhanced his development of the knowledge, skills, and attitudes being taught. What happens if we recognize learners as subjects? It can mean a radical change in our way of teaching. It can lead to radical changes in the effect of teaching: fewer dropouts, for example, as learners feel themselves respected and important decision makers in their own learning. It can mean more measurable results of the learning process, as learners know they know because they have chosen to do what they are learning. It can mean better use of financial and human resources, as adult learners practice making healthy decisions in the learning process. Joye Norris, a master of dialogue education, tells of the powerful results she has seen when learners are invited to "raise their own voices" and hear themselves, often for the first time. Paulo Freire, Brazilian educator, titled one of his books *Cultural Action for Freedom* (1970). Inviting learners to be subjects of their own learning is indeed the practice of freedom.

Principle 7: Ideas, Feelings, Actions

Learning with the mind, emotions, and muscles and giving attention to the cognitive, affective, and psychomotor aspects of adult learning is a vital principle that is often neglected. When the formalities of teaching and learning in the classroom and university take over without reflection, adult learners can be faced with a mass of cognitive matter: information, data, and facts that may seem impossible to comprehend or learn. When I took my first computer course, I had the personal experience of being deluged with facts about the history and emerging complexity of computers. I simply wanted to know how to use one. The mass of information frightened me away and I became another statistic: another adult learner who began a course and then dropped out.

Using the principle that there are three aspects of learning: ideas (cognitive), feelings (affective), and actions (psychomotor), we can prevent that initial fear at the outset of a new adult learning event.

We know that learning involves more than cognitive material (ideas and concepts). It involves feeling something about the concepts (emotions) and doing something (actions). Whether I am learning the concept of *stakeholders* in strategic planning, or the skill of playing the piano, or the attitude of confidence when addressing an audience, I need to consider all three aspects of learning: cognitive, affective, psychomotor.

The concept of preparing an agenda for a meeting, for example, certainly has affective overtones for someone learning how to have an effective meeting. Who is deciding the agenda? As soon as we consider the political implications of making an agenda and preparing a meeting, we can then practice doing it consciously. The more frequently I actually design an agenda, the more fully I grasp the concept. In this example, to learn the idea I have used a cognitive approach (defining an agenda), a psychomotor approach (designing it), and an affective approach (considering the implications of the power of the one who prepares the meeting). Kurt Lewin taught that little substantive learning takes place without involving something of all three aspects (Johnson and Johnson, 1991). Zohar shows the human self as mental, emotional, and spiritual and demonstrates how a holistic view of the world invites us constantly to consciously address all levels (1997, p. 10). Real change requires a fundamental shift at each of the three levels. This can be accomplished by designing learning tasks that have cognitive, affective, and psychomotor components (Vella, 2000).

The formal approaches to learning often assume that the cognitive aspect is everything. Joseph Campbell has a startling insight: "The brain thinks it is running the show. It isn't really. It is a peripheral organ, secondary at best!" (Campbell, 1988, p. 142).

In the Zambian example (Chapter Ten), church leaders who have struggled long and hard with the concept of equality, and who preach it, got a unique chance to feel it and do something with it. The results, to say the least, are interesting. Note the power relations addressed in that vivid experience of doing what they were learning. The design challenge in that chapter invites you to study your own educational projects in terms of cognitive, affective, and psychomotor possibilities (ideas, feelings, and actions) that address the whole person, not as a machine but as a developing man or woman, with incredible potential.

Principle 8: Immediacy

Research recognizes that adult learners need to see the immediate usefulness of new learning: the skills, knowledge, or attitudes they are working to acquire. Most adults do not have time to waste. We want to spend our time studying content that will make a difference *now*. We are willing to work in an appropriate sequence, and we recognize the need for reinforcement, but we want to see something in hand as soon as possible. A large percentage of adult learners start a course and then decide to give it up because they cannot see the immediate usefulness of what they are learning. Such immediacy is not a quick fix in a mechanistic sense. It is perceived usefulness, related to respect for the learner's context, sequence of learning tasks, and the data shared in the needs assessment. The immediacy perceived by learners will affect their determination to continue working. In quantum thinking, perception evokes reality. We participate in making our world.

How does this principle translate into practice? In designing a time management course for middle managers at a large factory, for example, a teacher uses the principle of immediacy by designing three short sessions instead of a day-long course. She makes sure the managers have one particular skill to practice at their posts in between these short sessions. When that skill makes a difference in the management of their usual activities, they gain confidence in the course, the teacher, and their own learning ability. A question we can offer at the end of each learning session is, *How can you use this new skill most effectively?* So learners, again as subjects, decide on the significance and application of the new skill.

The principle of immediacy helped the teacher decide how to organize the sessions in that short course. This offers an immediate example of what we mean by a principle: the beginning of an action. We are guided in the design of that course by the simple principle of immediacy. The principle of honoring learners as subjects would have us asking learners after the three short sessions: *How else could we have organized the time in this time management course? Let's use the very principles we've just learned to redesign this course!* That is using the principle of reinforcement as well as immediacy. As we develop skills in the use of all the principles and practices of dialogue education, we shall see how deeply intertwined they are. You can hardly use one without using all the others. The whole is greater than the sum of its parts. Each part contains the whole. *That* is quantum thinking.

In the war-torn streets of the little town of Due Arroyo in El Salvador (Chapter Eleven), the community organizers studying the principles and practices of community education had more than enough immediacy. The story shows how they applied what they were learning wisely enough to save their lives and mine.

Principle 9: Clear Roles

Another vital principle of adult learning is recognition of the impact of clear roles in the communication between learner and teacher. As Paulo Freire put it in conversation with us one evening: "Only the student can name the moment of the death of the professor." That is, a teacher can be intent upon a dialogue with an adult learner, but if the learner sees the teacher as "the professor" with whom there is no possibility of disagreement, no questioning, no challenge, the dialogue is dead in the water. Adult students need reinforcement of the human equity between teacher and student and among students. It takes time for adults to see themselves and the teacher in a new role.

In rural African villages, my colleague and I, two women, spent a lot of time walking around, talking to the mothers, holding their babies before teaching our leadership course. We swapped recipes in their kitchens and spent time watching them weave palm. The women always enjoyed our brave and clumsy efforts when we tried to weave and patiently tried to demonstrate the skill to us again and again. When we started to teach them, we had a significant new role as learners.

Before beginning a recent program with a national literacy organization, I spent time asking all the senior managers about their most recent discoveries in literacy education. "Dr. Vella" was soon transformed into "Jane"—a fellow searcher for ways to teach literacy, a woman who was interested in their work and their discoveries. I included myself somehow in their work by making telephone calls for learning needs and resources assessment and simply by asking: "What's new? What should I know about your present work?" This listening process established some equity in our roles.

Role is a delicate cultural issue. In some situations around the world—as a woman in a Muslim country such as Sudan, for example—it was vital to be "Dr. Vella" the whole time. In other situations, a first-name basis moved us toward dialogue. What's in a name? We wish to move adults to learn together in dialogue. Whatever impedes that dialogue must be courageously addressed and eradicated. Whatever enables that dialogue must be fearlessly nurtured and used. Accessibility is an issue here. If the teacher's perceived role does not lend itself to dialogue, learners will not seek her out. If the teacher is committed to a role that moves both toward dialogue, she will make sure there is time for dialogue both inside and outside the classroom. Time spent with learners at a party or at a dinner in a different role makes a big difference in their freedom to ask the disturbing question, disagree with a point, or venture a novel opinion from their unique context. Danah Zohar has a delightful phrase to describe how that freedom looks in a learning dialogue: "You hear a chorus of conversations!" (Zohar, 1997, p.143). I would add: a chorus of conversations in which learners are recreating the content you are teaching them so that it fits their context.

Role clarification and the move toward dialogue are never a cosmetic issue: they are both a matter of the heart and the heart of the matter. A graduate student recently suggested that another name for this principle is humility. In the graduate school of theology in New York (Chapter Twelve), we see professional men and women struggling toward dialogue, examining their roles with learners and with one another. This story tells how they found new meaning in the concept of *dia + logos*, "the word or relationship between us," as they found new roles and new relationships with their graduate students and with one another in dialogue education.

Principle 10: Teamwork

Teamwork is itself both a process and a principle. Teams provide, in the adult learning experience, a quality of safety that is effective and helpful. The assurance of safety and shared responsibility available in teams has always proved welcome, no matter what the cultural setting. Teamwork cannot be taken for granted. Through the learning needs and resources assessment, the teacher can take advice about the formation of teams. People can be invited to work with friends when possible. This provides safety for undertaking the difficult tasks. The concept of optimal field works for us here. An *optimal field* is one designed for everyone to gain as much as possible, one where we design for a win-win situation by intentionally including everything in the field that makes for success. Respecting people as subjects means having people choose their own teams as often as possible, especially when the learning task is complex and difficult. You can set up arbitrary teams at the beginning of a course and then have people form work teams for themselves, choosing with whom they wish to work. At times gender, age, or race are serious considerations in naming teams.

All too often we hear people in educational settings say: "When we get back to the real world. . . ." Teams *are* the real world. Team efforts in a learning situation are not vicarious and they are not contrived. What happens in the team is what is happening every day. As adult educators we must remember that feelings are never simulated. If an adult feels overwhelmed and excluded in a small group of people, those feelings are real. That adult will act out of those feelings of fear or exclusion throughout the course either by not returning or by disturbing the learning of all involved. The teacher must design for the inclusion of all.

This is exquisitely quantum thinking: nothing in the universe grows or develops alone. We learn together. We live in a participatory universe (Zohar, 1997, p. 68).

I have in the past described teams as limit situations, naturally imperfect. Today, from the perspective of the new science and quantum thinking, the dichotomy perfect-imperfect makes no sense. We are creating a world, a social, economic, cultural entity in an ordered universe that is naturally participatory. Reality is what we create. Do we dare use these principles to create, as Paulo Freire put it (1972, p. ix), a world where it is easier to love?

In a team, learning is enhanced by peers. We know that peers hold significant authority with adults, even more authority than teachers. Peers often have similar experiences. They can challenge one another in ways a teacher cannot. Peers create safety for the learner who is struggling with complex concepts, skills, or attitudes. I have seen significant mentoring go on in teams: peers helping one another, often with surprising clarity, tenderness, and skill.

Teams invite the welcome energy of competition. If we look at this word *competition*, we can see opportunity: *com* means "with," *petition* means "asking." We are asking together. There can, of course, be destructive competition among teams in a win-lose situation.

Constructive competition is structured so that teams work together in the learning process, manifesting their learning with a certain pride in their achievement as a team, in a win-win situation.

Teams examine another new potential in the learning situation, however, as different people learn how to work together generously and efficiently. We need time at the beginning of a course to invite learners to examine their roles in the team. There are group maintenance roles and task maintenance roles (Vella, 1995, p. 125). As a team considers how these roles are being acted out, they can name ways their team can work more efficiently. When learning tasks are deeply related to themes and time is adequate for the task, adult learners will work energetically in teams.

There can be an apparent contradiction between a learner's accountability to his personal objectives and his accountability to the team. When, in rare cases, a learner shows indifference or reluctance to join in a task, it is the teacher's responsibility to step in and work with that person. Perhaps the person should not be in the learning session at all. This is a decision to be made by both the adult learner and the teacher. The principle of safety is operative here. And that involves respect for the individual, for the teacher, and for the entire group.

The challenging story of team development in Zimbabwe (Chapter Thirteen) is unusual. Prior to the literacy training program, these young men and women had been members of military units in the guerrilla army that fought for Zimbabwe's independence. Now they were learning to be literacy coordinators with an entirely new idea of teamwork and a profoundly different purpose. This was a quantum leap for these young people.

Principle 11: Engagement

In Chapter Fourteen we see how a Hospice team's engagement in the learning and action plans for a strategic planning session was a vital principle to ensure the quality of the team's learning. Through learning tasks we invited learners to engage themselves actively in the strategic issues of their organizations and of the community.

This is exquisite quantum thinking: learning as a process of a participative universe. Mechanistic thinking allows us to be passive learners. Zohar quotes Frederick Taylor, a mechanistic organization specialist, to demonstrate how Newtonian thinking affects organizations. Taylor said, "Employees are passive units of production" (Zohar, 1997, p.69). When we do not use dialogue and instead ask learners to be passive, they do indeed learn. They learn how to be passive, to be "good" employees. They learn that they have no power, except to obey. This is not the goal of adult learning in my perspective.

When learners are deeply engaged, working in small groups or teams, it is often difficult to extricate them from the delight of that learning. The director of that Hospice wisely invited complete engagement from all quarters. There were no levels of participation; everyone took part in the needs assessment and strategic planning. You will notice that some Hospice staff who were on holiday actually came to the program. *That* is quantum engagement.

Principle 12: Accountability

Accountability is one of the foremost principles of adult learning. Earlier in this chapter I spoke of it in terms of sequence and reinforcement. Who is accountable to whom? First, the design of learning events must be accountable to the learners. What was proposed to be taught must be taught; what was meant to be learned must be learned; the skills intended to be gained must be visible in all the learners; the attitudes taught must be seen; the knowledge conveyed must be manifest in adult learners' language and reasoning. Second, the learners in teams are accountable to their colleagues and to the teacher. They are accountable to themselves to recreate the content so it really is immediately useful in their context. Accountability is a synthesis principle—it is the result of using all the other principles.

Chapter Fifteen is about a training event with doctors in Bangladesh. It offers a surprising example of the need for accountability. This story relates also to the issue of role. The doctors in the training program had a very hard time accepting that they needed to learn how to teach. Their role in their own country is such that they receive little personal or professional feedback on their teaching skills. As they learned the principles and practiced them among themselves, they found their role changing.

Ancient hierarchical relationships do not lend themselves to dialogue. They are reminiscent of the hierarchical system of the medieval state and church that we inherited and shaped into systems in industry, school, university, and government. This hierarchy was corroborated by a worldview of the universe and all that is in it as a vast machine. That worldview has an alternative, since Niels Bohr in 1923 split the atom and discovered within, not more matter, but energy. The measure of energy, a quanta, was named in 1905 by Einstein. Quantum physics presents a new perception of the universe and of our role in it. The kind of thinking needed to understand quantum physics is the key to understanding the whole new paradigm that is emerging (Zohar, 1997, p. 43). This quantum thinking leads to new and deeper accountability.

I have always tried, through careful design and through the use of the principles of dialogue education, to be accountable to learners. Today, using quantum thinking, I can be accountable in a new way: aware that what learners learn is much beyond what I have planned. The quantum concept of their participation in the construction of meaning and usefulness assures me. They are learning what they need for their context. I can review their portfolios and see how they have constructed appropriate meaning from the content I offered for their life and work. That is quantum accountability.

Thomas Kuhn offers us a useful hypothesis: change of a pattern, which he calls a paradigm shift, will only occur when the present pattern has proven itself ineffective and impossible to live with (Kuhn, 1970, p. 18). Part of my job in this book is to contrast patterns and demonstrate how inefficient the hierarchical, mechanistic pattern is when we are attempting to teach adults. If we are insensitive to the cultural perspectives and value systems of the people we teach, we will not succeed in designing and effecting a dialogue with them. Dialogue does not serve those who see human beings as machines in a mechanistic universe.

As we work in our complex global and national society to reach adults who need knowledge, skills, and new, healthier attitudes to build healthy lives and we see those adults as subjects of their own lives, we can accountably design for dialogue. The basic assumption is that all learners come with both experience and personal perceptions of the world based on that experience and all deserve respect as subjects of a learning dialogue. Adult education, community education, and training are most effective when we honor that assumption. This is quantum thinking at its best. This is dialogue education. The twelve chapters of Part Two offer stories of adult learning situations based on such dialogue education.

2

Quantum Thinking and
Dialogue Education

Quantum thinking means looking at the world in a new way, based on the century-long work of physicists and other scientists who moved beyond classical or Newtonian mechanics to the new paradigm of quantum physics. In this chapter I will show how I see dialogue education and quantum thinking working together.

Since September 11, 2001, we are living in a new world where the search for practical new paradigms in every discipline is urgent. As a septuagenarian educator, I see the need to revise and reform educational practice and policy as even more urgent. How we work and live in an educational setting is a powerful force in developing how we live and work in the world.

Classical Newtonian physics has touched and formed all our institutions: economic, educational, organizational, political. We have been brought up to accept hierarchy, certainty, cause-and-effect relationships, either-or thinking, and a universe that works as a machine—in short, mechanistic thinking. It is a shock for most of us to consider a universe composed of energy that is patterned and spontaneous, the certainty of uncertainty, "both/and" thinking, and the connectedness of everything. This is quantum thinking.

I appreciate the application of such quantum thinking by Margaret Wheatley and Danah Zohar to organizational development and management practices. The more I read in quantum physics and quantum theory, the more I saw the connection between what

I call quantum thinking and the humanistic, integrated approach of dialogue education. In the 1994 edition of this book I called this approach popular education, building it from the foundation laid by the Brazilian educator, Paulo Freire. In this revised edition, I want to show how dialogue education is congruent with the kind of thinking about the universe and about men and women and society that emerges from the study of quantum theory. In this chapter I will show some connections between the principles of dialogue education and selected concepts from quantum thinking. My intention is not to teach quantum theory, of course, but to excite you about the usefulness of quantum thinking in the design and implementation of dialogue education. The six quantum concepts I have selected relate to dialogue education.

Newton's view of the universe and all it contains as a vast machine with many parts, some of which are more important than others, emerged from seventeenth century Europe, where an incipient industrial revolution was changing society. The machine was central; therefore, a universe that was a vast machine was a congruent concept.

That worldview has an alternative, however, since physicists split the atom and discovered within it, not more matter, but energy. The measure of energy is a quanta. Quantum physics offers a radically new perception of the universe and our role in it.

Dialogue education, as I perceive it and have taught it, is informed by quantum concepts—ideas that emerge from the worldview of quantum physics. I have selected these six:

- *Relatedness:* All that we do in design and teaching is related. Each of the twelve principles is related to all the others.

- A *holistic perspective:* The whole is far more than the sum of its parts. Learners learn more than we teach!

- *Duality:* Embrace opposites, use both/and thinking. Open questions invite both/and thinking and dialogue.

- *Uncertainty:* Every theory is constantly being constructed by application to new contexts.

- *Participation:* The observer is part of what she observes. Each person's perception of any given reality is different, dependent on their context and culture. We evoke the world we perceive.

- *Energy:* Learning demands energy. Many of the principles and practices of dialogue education are designed to raise and sustain the energy of learners.

Throughout this revised edition in each of the stories teaching the principles, I will show how the twelve selected principles of dialogue education mesh with these six selected concepts from quantum thinking.

Classical, hierarchical education uses classical concepts: not relatedness but separateness, for example. Think of education, where science and art are separate, research in one discipline is hoarded and not shared with others, and forty-five minute "periods" separate out the disciplines. A mechanistic world view holds an "atomistic" perspective, which sees the whole as merely the sum of its parts. Consider a testing system that is based on closed questions. That is what emerges from an atomistic perspective. An educational philosophy that is based on rigid black-and-white norms and that presents either-or data reflects classical Newtonian thinking. Such thinking precludes a constructionist perspective that invites learners to develop the theory they are learning in light of their own context.

Consider the absolute certainty of many educational systems: This is the way it is! Uncertainty is an anathema. Such an educational system says: What I am teaching is doctrine, indisputable, sure. Instead of the participation that honors the effect of context and culture on a learner's perspective, this mechanistic approach demands a strict objectivity. Consider how educational systems are affected by such a seventeenth century, materialist perspective, which stresses product over process. It is the source of an educational curriculum that prepares young men and women merely for the world of work, not for the work of the world, which is discovery, creation, integration, peace making.

Principles and Practices and Quantum Concepts

The purpose of dialogue education is to evoke optimal learning with adults. It is designed from a set of assumptions about the nature of society and human beings—assumptions embodied in the principles and practices and corollary quantum concepts.

1. *Learning Needs and Resources Assessment.* Doing a learning needs and resources assessment honors the context of the learners. This is directly related to the holistic worldview of quantum thinking. The whole situation of learners affects our decisions about *what* to teach and *how* to teach it. This principle and practice of needs assessment also uses the quantum concepts of participation and energy. Learners who have had the opportunity to speak to their expectations of a curriculum will bring their perspective to the course and will have high energy about their learning. In a learning needs and resources assessment we as designers and instructors can see the relatedness of what we hope to teach to the context of the adult learners.

2. *Safety.* When we create a safe context for learning that is appropriate for adults and we challenge them accordingly, we can see the energy in the group rise. We provide a site for learners to explore the uncertainty of any skill or theory, providing a safe place for the both/and thinking that is needed if their learning is to be relevant to their unique context. As they construct authentic the-

ory and practice from the content offered, their world can look chaotic. Safety is all the more needed when uncertainty is honored.

3. *Sound Relationships*. Sound relationships among learners and between learners and teacher reflect respect for the uniqueness of each person and the connection of all that occurs and all that is being studied. With affirmation and challenge, the energy of adult learners is unleashed. Since in quantum thinking we evoke the world we perceive, adult learners, perceived as respected and competent by a caring educator, can become what they are perceived as being. This is an extraordinary statement, one that is possible only with quantum thinking, and it has been corroborated often by my experience. We know it as the power of trust.

4. *Sequence of Content and Reinforcement*. As you maintain a holistic perspective on the content of your courses, you will see how that content can be sequenced and reinforced to fit the group of learners. Respect for the connection of everything within that content will enable you to offer parts of the content with an eye on the whole. Watch the energy of a group of adult learners rise when your learning tasks are well-sequenced and offer adequate reinforcement.

5. *Praxis*. When we can respect learners as subjects of their own life learning and turn them to learning tasks that invite their creation of viable theory, we are congruent with a number of the selected quantum concepts. Such an attitude involves respect for (1) the energy of learning, (2) duality (both/and thinking), (3) uncertainty, and (4) the learner as participant in the process of constructing theory.

6. *Respect for Learners as Decision Makers*. This principle is directly related to participation, the quantum concept that teaches us the uniqueness of each person's perception of what we are teaching. Learners will decide what works for them from the content. This principle relates also to energy. Notice how energy rises when learners are aware of their responsibility to decide.

7. *Learning with Ideas, Feelings, and Actions*. This principle relates directly to a holistic perception of the universe and whatever

we are teaching. It relates to participation and to the flow of energy needed for effective learning.

8. *Immediacy.* As we try to reach learners with content that is relevant and immediately useful, we are using the quantum concept of relatedness by recognizing the connection of all aspects of a course. Nothing is insignificant, but some things speak more directly to learners in their unique context. This principle also speaks to participation of learners who make new content work in their context.

9. *Clear Roles and Role Development.* As I strive to clarify my role as teacher in dialogue education, I am working within the quantum concepts of duality, energy, participation, and relatedness. I am both decision maker and listener. I respect the learners' energy level and challenge them to "push the envelope." I recognize that from their context the content I am teaching may look different, and I see that we are all together in the search for meaningful learning.

10. *Teamwork.* As I design learning tasks to engage learners in small groups, I am working in ways congruent with all six of the selected quantum concepts:

> *Relatedness and holistic perspective:* As team members work together they discover how connected they are, how their effort builds toward a whole.
>
> *Duality, energy:* The energy of the small group moves toward product through a focused process. Which is more important to the team? Product or process? Both . . . and!
>
> *Uncertainty, participation:* In a team it soon becomes clear that uncertainty is real. Differing perspectives often spell chaos, which moves to profound learning as learners from diverse contexts make content meaningful. These different perspectives show how subjective and idiosyncratic any learning is.

11. *Engagement.* When learners are engaged in what they are learning, again all six quantum concepts are involved. Especially

obvious is the concept of holism; engagement is not only cognitive but also affective and muscular.

12. *Accountability.* When we accept mutual responsibility for learning, we are using the quantum concept of holism and we see how everything we do and teach is related. Our awareness of the importance of accountability affects our own energy in the learning-teaching relationship. We listen to learners with more finely attuned ears.

The Whole Picture

These six quantum concepts are a tenuous wire on which to hang the connection of quantum thinking with dialogue education. But the quantum revolution is so profound, so radical, and so vital that I knew I could only offer a sample without making this revised edition a textbook on quantum epistemology. During the stories that follow, I will refer to other quantum concepts but focus on these six. When you begin to read the titles on quantum theory named in the Resources section, you will recognize how vast a study you have before you. Here we are examining but the tip of the iceberg to make a connection between dialogue education and the quantum thinking.

3

How the Principles
Inform Course Design
Two Examples

This chapter offers two examples that demonstrate how the twelve principles inform the design of adult education. The principles work equally well in both cases, although the settings, participants, and purposes of the courses are different. Both cases use the seven steps for design—who, why, when, where, what, what for, how—which I see as an essential tool for creating a flexible design that can ensure sound learning. In Vella (2000) you will find a detailed description of the seven steps and further opportunities to practice using them.

Example One: A Workshop for Conducting Effective Meetings

In the first example, a team of adult educators has been invited by a small not-for-profit organization to design and teach its staff and board members principles and practices for effective meetings. This organization lives from meeting to meeting, but the members find many of their meetings to be time-wasting.

The Seven Design Steps

Our use of the seven design steps—*who, why, when, where, what for, what,* and *how*—honors our respect for the learners as decision makers of this learning process. The seven steps focus the design and invite use of the twelve principles as we make our plan.

The initial question to be answered is *who*. Who are these learners? They will be the board and staff of the organization. We want to learn through the learning needs and resources assessment all we can of their present situation. We want to hear what they consider the immediate needs for learning about the topic. This particular organization is ten years old, with a board of seven men and women from prestigious community agencies. Board and staff need to learn these skills to ensure comprehensive participation not only in meetings but also in every aspect of their operation. Who needs what as defined by whom is the question at the heart of the learning needs and resources assessment. Another guiding question is, Who else needs to be here? This honors both the cross-cultural and political issues in the organization and the community it serves. How many learners will attend the session? When we have completed this first design step, we are clear about exactly who will be the learners and how many of them we can expect.

Another design question is *why*: Why does the present situation call for this course? Why are the named outcomes necessary? And what do the participants need to be able to do as a result of the course? We see that the agency needs information and skills about how to make its meetings work. Board meetings are often tense and stiff. The board is missing the verve and spontaneity that exist among the staff. The director needs a process and a set of guidelines for the many kinds of meetings she designs and runs—with the board, clients, the community, and fundraisers. Remembering the quantum principle that the whole is greater than the sum of its parts, we address the issue of meetings, knowing that deeper issues of relevance, inclusive participation, and shared values will also be a part of the dialogue.

As we examine the *who* and *why* questions, we use virtually all of the principles. The staff and board members themselves are respected as the decision makers of this course (subjects). The content must have immediate usefulness to them (immediacy). Their cultural perspectives are diverse and must be explicitly honored (respect). The roles among the group will have to be clarified and respected (clear roles). Safety will be ensured with adequate time together and a careful sequencing of tasks for the learners to do in small groups (safety, sequence). Learners will have reinforcement of what they are learning about designing and facilitating effective meetings as they use new skills in the course of the training session (reinforcement). The outcome of the short course is that they will be able to both design more effective meetings and take part in those meetings with greater engagement (engagement).

Other logistical questions invite us to honor these learners as decision makers of their own learning: *when* and *where*. It is vital to choose a time that is convenient for this unique group. The staff could come on a weekday, as part of their work, but the board members cannot. So the decision is a delicate one. The timing of a community education event is always a political decision. How can we decide on a time that honors the safety of all? The board and staff finally decide on a time when the greatest number can be present. For this question, participants have a deliberative voice: they make the decision about *when*.

The design question *when* invites serious consideration of just how much can be taught in the available time. In this case, the staff and board agree to a two-hour session. We set achievement based objectives and content appropriate to that time frame.

Where such an event occurs is another decision that involves many of the principles. Where a session is held speaks to the political value of inclusion (respect). We need an environment that feels safe for all and has room for small-group work at tables (safety). The environment also must be convenient and accessible to all the participants, many of whom use public transport. These considerations involve a synthesis of virtually all the principles, honoring the life situation or context of all the learners. The director polls the group and decides to hold the sessions in a church lounge near the office. People can get to it by foot since it is close to their homes.

The question that names the content of a course is *what*. In formal education, the professor usually begins planning by considering content. He names the skills, attitudes, and knowledge that will be imparted to the learners. In dialogue education, the adults' needs, discovered during the learning needs and resources assessment, inform the *what*. Guidelines for the design and facilitation of a good meeting are classic and clearly set out in the literature of organizational development. How those guidelines are interpreted and then organized, however, must be determined by the context. We finally decide, in conference with the director, that this group needs to practice using a comprehensive list of preparatory steps for designing an effective meeting. They also need to experience and reflect upon an efficient process.

The principles of immediacy and accountability oblige us to take the raw content of concepts, skills, and attitudes and weave it into a useful set of knowledge and skills for this particular group. The principle of praxis enables us to shape our plan so that members will do what they are learning and then examine from their own cultural perspective what they are doing, in teams, as decision makers. Such an approach frees the teacher to listen and design, set learning tasks that are accountable for achieving the set objectives, and teach the content without domination or cultural intrusion, since she is not the only decision maker. She will be able to respond using the language of the learners as they do the learning tasks. Adult learners know when they are being respected. The rise in energy and creativity is manifest in the group of learners when they discover *how* the design honestly invites their opinion and respects their life experience.

The content we decide to teach relates directly to the achievement based objectives. This is an iterative process: *what* (the content) is represented by nouns. The content of this particular two-hour workshop includes (1) classic issues that arise at meetings of nonprofit organizations, (2) sixteen guidelines for an effective meeting, and (3) the distinction between consultative and deliberative voices in a meeting.

The design step *what for* is expressed in achievement—based objectives that are represented by verbs, showing what the learners will do with that named content. We are mutually accountable to achieve the objectives before the end of this two-hour workshop. We honor the fact that learners must do something (psychomotor activity) with what they are learning if they are to know that they know. We offer the director a draft set of achievement based objectives based on our learning needs and resources assessment and our decision about content. It is her job to edit them and assure us as designers and teachers that we are on the right track.

Achievement Based Objectives and Outcomes

A common program planning practice is to state outcomes of a course in this way: *By the end of this workshop these participants will be able to design and lead effective meetings*. Such a statement of outcomes is necessary in the design of outcome-based education (OBE).

In South Africa OBE is a national priority. All training and adult education programs must name outcomes and measure success by them. My colleague Sarah Gravett of Johannesburg and I have worked long and hard to design a way to integrate OBE and the seven design steps, which work so well for accountability. We realized that outcomes can be included in the *why*—the situation— since they describe why learners need the skills, knowledge, and attitudes being taught. We therefore describe the present situation, which calls for the educational event, and then the outcomes. Achievement based objectives are not outcomes. Outcomes are not operative in program design because they are not specific enough to lead to learning tasks (Vella, 2000, p. 105). There is a direct link in this dialogue education approach between the situation (why), the content (what), the achievement based objectives (what for), and specific learning tasks and materials (how).

We set these specific achievement based objectives for this short workshop:

By the End of This Two-Hour
Workshop We All Will Have . . .

1. Named some issues we have with meetings

2. Examined a list of guideline questions

3. Added to that list

4. Named the guidelines that seem most useful

5. Practiced using at least one guideline

6. Distinguished between a consultative and a deliberative voice

Such achievement based objectives ensure accountability and honor the learners as decision makers of their own learning. Each objective is directly related to a content piece *(what)* and to one or more learning tasks *(how)* that will involve cognitive, affective, and psychomotor activities. The sequence of the achievement based objectives is related to the natural sequence of those tasks and each reinforces the previous learning.

The *how* is the action program: a set of sequenced learning tasks through which the staff and their board will, in teams, use the concepts they are learning to design and practice having an effective meeting. Learning tasks are open questions put to a small group for response with all the resources they need. In this case, each learning task had a worksheet of materials. As small groups completed the tasks, they shared their responses and we collated them. An effective meeting design emerged, step by step, as each new step reinforced the learning and decisions in the previous one.

What is the role of the teacher while learners are doing their learning tasks? Teachers are resources for the process and for the content. We invite questions and respond to them without giving a lengthy dissertation on the issue. Our central job is to prepare the design through our comprehensive use of the seven design steps and to set learning tasks in careful sequence. Once the learning starts, through the immediate praxis of the small groups, we get out of the way but stay available as resources for questions on process or content. "Sit still, keep quiet, pay attention": this is indeed a new role for the "professor."

It is our job to collate and organize the responses of the groups when their tasks are completed. During this collation there is often occasion for our responses: linking one point with another, showing significant differences in points of view, sharing related experiences from similar groups, making corrections where the perception of learners is distorted. While learners enjoy this commentary, teachers must realize that this is not the only learning time. Students have been learning throughout the task. If our commentary, coming from another cultural perspective, does not seem reasonable to them, they will object to it or question it. Their objections are a vital part of the dialogue, clarifying both the materials and the tasks. It is important for the teacher to ask the open question, *What are your questions about this synthesis?*

The next section outlines the tasks we set for this program on effective meetings and the materials we shared with students, including the critical incident, a case study that raises an immediate issue. Note that the case study is set out as a critical incident in order to evoke the affective response of the group and to bring that energy to bear in their learning. Paulo Freire in the early 1970s spoke of "problem-posing education" (1972, p. 74). This was a big step forward from a monologue that offered answers before questions were named. Quantum thinking, however, looks not at problems, but rather at potential within contexts, inviting learners to use their creativity and imagination to perceive viable alternatives.

"We've Got to Stop Meeting Like This"

This is a sample of a two-hour workshop in which the seven design steps and all the principles and practices we have been reviewing were used.

The Seven Design Steps

• *Who* (participants). Eighteen staff and board members of a ten-year-old nonprofit group involved in providing meals for elderly citizens.

• *Why* (present situation). At present group members hold many meetings and see them as a waste of time. They need to make their meetings more effective. Outcome: They will be able to design and lead effective meetings (outcome).

• *When* (time frame). Thursday evening for two hours, from 7 to 9 P.M.

• *Where* (site). Church lounge: a room with comfortable chairs for twenty people, tables to work at, and wall space for charts.

• *What* (content: skills, knowledge, attitudes). Classic problems that arise at meetings of nonprofit organizations; sixteen guidelines for an effective meeting; the distinction between consultative and deliberative voices in a meeting.

• *What for* (achievement based objectives). By the end of this two-hour workshop, we will have named some issues we have about our meetings, examined a list of guidelines for an effective meeting, and made the distinction between deliberative and consultative voices in a meeting.

• *How* (learning needs and resources assessment, learning tasks and materials). Materials: a case study and a set of sixteen guidelines for effective meetings. Learning needs and resources assessment: this draft program will be sent by e-mail to a sample of four (two staff, two board members) for their review and suggestions for changes.

Program

Learning Task #1: Program Review and Warm-Up

1. Listen to and review the seven design steps for this evening's workshop.

2. Name at your table one thing about meetings in this organization that you take issue with. We'll hear all.

Learning Task #2: A Typical Meeting in Trouble

1. Read this case study of a troubled meeting in Chicago. At your table express your response to it.

2. Read the set of guidelines for the preparation, facilitation, and recording of a meeting. Circle those guidelines that you see would have made that Chicago meeting more effective. We'll share a sample of your responses.

Learning Task #3: Application to Our Situation

1. Which items in this set do you see are most important for your meetings here?

2. What would you add to this list? We will share all that you offer.

Case Study: A Troubled Meeting

Here is a typical situation in a busy not-for-profit agency in Chicago. A critical meeting has been called by the agency director for 4 P.M. He announced the meeting at the 11 A.M. coffee break that morning. It is Friday, December 19. There is an agenda that the director has prepared. It has twelve items on it. When people arrive somewhat reluctantly at 4 P.M., they discover that the director is not present. He was called to a critical meeting by his boss upstairs, who directs the Chicago Coalition.

The meeting finally begins at 4:20 when the director arrives, a bit breathless from running. He does not have the materials he needs to distribute to staff for item 1 on his agenda. A resource person from the Coalition has been invited to discuss budget issues with the staff. This budget specialist has not been briefed adequately. She does not understand that decisions on budget are made not by the staff but by the director and the board. The writing on the blackboard is hardly legible because the room is dark on the wintry Friday afternoon. No one has been designated recorder of the meeting, so when the blackboard is erased, the many points recorded there are lost.

The meeting ends abruptly when the director is called out for an important phone call from a national foundation about a proposal due to them on Monday. There is no indication when this group will meet again. People go home quite dispirited.

A Set of Guidelines: Questions to Ask

Preparation

1. Has an agenda been prepared for the meeting?

2. Has this agenda been shared beforehand with all who are to be involved in the meeting? How long beforehand?

3. Is this meeting really necessary, or could the information be shared in another, less expensive, way?

4. Have the resource people been fully informed about the participants, the purpose of the meeting, their presentation time, and their expected role in the meeting?

5. Does everyone have minutes of the last meeting so that there is continuity?

6. Have all the materials for the meeting been gathered— documents, audiovisual support, and so forth?

The Meeting Itself

7. Is it clear who the chairperson or facilitator of the meeting is?

8. Is time sufficient for all tasks on the agenda?

9. Does everyone present have all the necessary materials?

10. Are people clear about the difference between a consultative voice (a suggestion) and a deliberative voice (a decision)?

11. Has a recorder or secretary been appointed to keep a record?

12. What about the meeting room? Lights? Space? Table room? Blackboard or easel and flip-chart? Audiovisual apparatus?

13. Does the facilitator or chairperson move briskly from item to item on the agenda?

14. How does the group deal with an obtrusive member, that is, one who is not cooperating with the process of the meeting?

15. Are all the participants feeling good about their opportunity to speak during the meeting? That is, is the meeting fully open?

16. How are questions for clarification asked? How are substantive questions on the issue asked? Do people see the difference?

Feedback

Learning task #4 is a feedback task. We invite feedback on the design of the program with this question: What was most useful to you in this two-hour session? Your response not only offers feedback to program designers and teachers, but also summarizes the learning experience of all.

———

Learning is what occurs in the two-hour session. Transfer will occur when the group uses these new skills and new knowledge in the design and process of their next meeting. Impact is the change the organization will feel as a function of more efficient, effective meetings (Vella and others, 1998).

Example Two: A Training Course for National Service Staff

In the next example, we see the preparation and design of a training program for National Service (NS) staff who are about to teach young recruits how to work in small rural communities.

The Seven Design Steps

- *Who* (participants). There are sixteen young men and women in this course. All are recent graduates of small colleges and most have majored in sociology, community development, or psychology. They are NS staff who will be teaching recruits how to work in small rural communities. This design will be a model for future training. The course members will be working with similar groups of sixteen in future NS staff training programs. Teachers: Two NS staff experienced in dialogue education.

- *Why*. The present situation: the situation that calls for this training course is obvious—these graduates will soon be teaching hundreds of young National Service staff members how to work productively with small rural communities. Since the participants have just come from a formal university setting, it is vital that they learn a new way of teaching to use with the NS staff. They need to learn an alternative to the familiar, more formal teaching approach of the university. Outcome: The participants will be able to design and teach with a dialogue approach.

- *When* (the time frame). This is a two-week program, including some class work and intensive fieldwork in a small rural community in Missouri. We have seventy hours of work together.

- *Where*. The training takes place at a community training center near a small agricultural town in rural Missouri.

- *What* (content). Theories of adult learning, the difference between monologue and dialogue, a theory of communication, how to do a community needs and resources assessment, the seven design steps, the principles and practices of dialogue education, how to complete record forms for the National Service agency.

- *What for* (achievement based objectives). By the end of the two weeks, all sixteen participants will have examined theories of adult learning, distinguished between monologue and dialogue, examined communication theories, practiced doing a community needs assessment, examined the principles and practices of dialogue education as they are modeled in this course, practiced designing training programs for NS staff by using the seven design steps and all the principles and practices of dialogue education, read and reviewed a selected set of books and articles on community education and dialogue education, practiced specific communication skills in the field, set criteria for communication between NS staff and the community, practiced active listening in the community, completed a set of record forms for the NS office. These objectives will be achieved through the set of learning tasks.

• *How*. Learning needs and resources assessment (LNRA), learning tasks, and materials.

This program, learning tasks, and materials will be presented to the sixteen participants before they come to the course. That includes the achievement based objectives. Teachers will speak to the participants by phone or via e-mail to hear their response to the program design.

The learning needs and resources assessment for this training involves a conversation with each learner, asking them what their perceived needs are in relation to the new job. It is likely that the teacher will hear they want to learn how to teach the new NS staff effectively and to practice meeting the community and working with them. They will undoubtedly express concern about the NS paperwork. Many will say they want a sure sense of what the goals and objectives of the National Service program are.

This learning needs and resources assessment helps us determine which objective takes priority. Our doing this needs assessment with them can lead to their doing such a needs assessment with the community. We know we are modeling a new way of teaching.

What follows is a small sample of the learning tasks they will perform to achieve a few of the objectives. The first content piece, theories of adult learning, is taught by this learning task.

Learning Task: How Adults Learn

In groups of threes, describe the best learning experience in your life. Analyze that experience. What were the factors that made you learn? After we review your factors, we will compare them with this summary of factors named by Malcolm Knowles and his associates when doing research on adult learning (Knowles, 1970). They discovered that adults learn when they feel themselves respected, the new learning is related to their life experience, and the new learning has some immediate usefulness to them. Moreover, they learn most effectively what they do or discover for themselves.

As the sixteen participants assess their own learning, analyze it, and then compare the factors that enabled them to learn with those named by adult education specialists, they come to trust their own experience and to feel self-respect and respect for the perspective of their colleagues. By the end of this learning task, the young people will have named all the factors discovered by the researchers in Knowles's work. A final open question invites them to apply their discoveries to both the training they will do with NS staff and their work in the community: "How can this knowledge of how adults learn help you in your work in the community and with the new National Service staff?"

The small groups provide safety, as the young adults can speak openly with three or four of their peers. The informal design of the room, with tables for groups of three or four, breaks down the stereotype of formal classroom relationships. The small groups can quickly become learning teams, working together to help one another reflect and learn and building a spirit of constructive competitiveness in the room.

The achievement based objective of completing the record forms for the government office can be met by the following learning task:

Learning Task: Watch Your Form!

Read the list of community events led by National Service staff. At your tables, complete the record sheet to reflect all the work done that week. Directions for filling out the form are there for you. Use us as resources to answer any of your questions. Share your completed forms with one other table after ten minutes. What are your questions?

———————

This learning task invites all participants to act as decision makers of their own learning, work as a team, teach one another, monitor one another, and suggest changes. The role of the teacher has changed dramatically here. Our job is to design the list of events, set the tasks, and be available as a resource when learners have questions. We will review each table's NS report form and help students with parts that are obscure or ambiguous. Honoring and respecting adults as decision makers in their own learning uncovers endless sources of energy for cooperation. We have often found that suggestions from the learners about such technical tasks are often innovative and creative and can make the task less difficult for all involved. Useful suggestions for revision of NS report forms can arise from such dialogue. The teacher is also learning.

Later learning tasks will take the NS trainers into the community and invite them to assess and analyze their involvement. Sequence and reinforcement are at work in our setting such tasks after we have done serious work on basic learning and communication theory. Our efforts are not designed to test; they are designed to teach. When adults have adequate reinforcement and are invited to use a skill, knowledge, or attitude in the community, they usually can do it well.

In this National Service training course we have insisted on sixteen participants so that we can get to know each one and can establish a sound relationship for learning. During the two-week course, the instructor is a resource, an advocate, a counselor. In an adult learning situation like this, the formal distance between teacher and student that one might recall from school days is not helpful. If we want a learning dialogue to occur, we must establish a safe environment for that dialogue.

The group will have learned that respect is the most important variable in adult learning. Recruits will then go out to the community for an initial set of meetings. As they try to show respect for the midwestern farmers they meet at the Parent Teachers Association, grange meetings, and county extension seminars, they have the tools for praxis, for analyzing their encounters. Each time they go out, they will notice that their efforts are more professional, more effective. Community people will feel they are being listened to, being heard. That word gets around a Missouri town very quickly!

We will have been explicit about the cross-cultural situation here, asking in the training course: How do you spell respect in rural Missouri? The teaching staff will have read and studied a great deal about this modern agricultural society and its current economic and ecological issues. They will have invited learners to spend time at the open market, the shopping mall in town, the library, the city hall, and various organizational meetings, introducing themselves and talking with citizens. Such learning tasks involve ideas, actions, and feelings. When learning tasks involve all three aspects, they work. The new staff of NS will teach the National Service staff they train in the same way, aware that adult learning always involves more than cognitive content; it involves affective and psychomotor activities as well.

Throughout the training course, the men and women are fully engaged in learning tasks in their teams in the classroom and in the community. Their engagement is ensured by the immediacy of the learning task, which relates to the immediacy of the course objective that the task is implementing. Without this engagement, learners simply cannot learn. Our job is to design effective achievement based objectives with corresponding learning tasks and materials. When we do this well, we are in fact accountable to the young NS recruits and can assure them that they will learn what we have set out for them to learn. They will know they know at the end of the two-week period. Such accountability is never accidental. It is ensured by design.

Since this training course is in fact a training of trainers, and the sixteen participants will be teaching what they have just learned to new NS staff members, transfer will be immediately possible. The participants will design parts of a training program to use with new staff and then lead parts of that program in teams of two, teaching their colleagues. We will videotape their teaching and offer them feedback on both the design and their teaching skills.

In Part Two, you will read stories showing how the twelve principles of adult learning were significant in the design and teaching of a course for a particular group of people. My experience and reflection have convinced me that these principles, given a fair chance, are universal.

Part II

The Principles in Practice
Across Cultures and Around the World

4

Learning Needs and
Resources Assessment
Taking the First Step in Dialogue

In Chapter One you read about learning needs and resources assessment (LNRA). You saw that it is a process through which the
teacher learns and then makes explicit for learners their themes, issues, and questions around the topic being taught. Surveys, on-site
visits, informal sessions such as potluck suppers, and telephone or
e-mail interviews can be used with a sample of the learning group
to get a sense of the learners' real situation. Tom Hutchinson's
WWW question is always useful: *Who* needs *what* as defined by
whom? (Hutchinson, 1978). In the story told in this chapter, watch
how the learning needs and resources assessment informed what was
taught in staff development training. Notice how the LNRA in this
particular case occurred with the participants during the first days
of the training session.

How do you set learning objectives in a strange land, in a strange
language, for an unprecedented relief and development activity?
How do you teach a group of Ethiopian youth and an Afar nomad
woman to implement a relief program responsibly? How do you do
this under intense time pressure, with over half a million lives depending on the knowledge and skills of the young staff? Who are
the natural definers of these learning objectives: the teacher? The
program directors? Government officials? The learners themselves?

How do you select, from all the conflicting objectives you hear, those that can be achieved in the available time? How do you assure accountability and quality in the performance of the young staff?

The Situation

You may recall the evening when Tom Brokaw of NBC news shocked millions of Americans at their dinner tables by presenting a raw picture of a ravaging drought in northern Ethiopia. Before the evening news program was over, telephones were ringing at Save the Children offices in Westport, Connecticut, with offers of financial support from sympathetic men and women all over the country. People had rarely been so touched and so moved to offer whatever they could to stop the horrific hunger they had witnessed on that ninety-second TV clip. Save the Children Foundation USA (SCF) had no program at that time in Ethiopia. It was their British colleagues in the TV film who had touched the hearts of people around the world. As funds for Ethiopia flooded in, decisions were made to set up an SCF program as quickly as possible.

By early December, the government of Ethiopia had named an area in which SCF could focus efforts at relief and development. It was Yfrat and Timuga, a district with one town called Epheson, seven hours north of Addis Ababa. A medical doctor and a manager were in Addis setting up the program with the Ethiopian government as international groups coordinated the relief services. The staff of the new program were to be recruited and hired in the area and then trained there before starting work. As director of training, I was sent to Ethiopia to design and lead their training. I was responsible to the American director of the Ethiopian program to get the staff into action as soon as possible with all the skills and knowledge they would need to manage a multimillion dollar operation.

I knew nothing about Ethiopia and little about the drought that I had not read in the daily papers. How could I prepare myself to teach the Ethiopian people who might be hired for this program? Further, I had no idea what skills and knowledge I would be teaching, since it was still not clear what the program was going to look like. Both the director of primary health and the Ethiopian program director were determined to avoid opening another relief station where mothers brought starving babies in to die before dying themselves. What was the alternative? Dr. Warren Berggren, the project physician, knew he had a viable alternative.

Resources were abundant, thanks to the generosity of Americans touched by the horrors of the drought. How could we use these resources wisely and teach Ethiopian staff to do the same? How could we make these resources stretch beyond the relief effort into a brighter, drought-free development phase? The doctor had a plan. He intended, drawing on his long experience in Zaire and Haiti, to put into place a relief program that would bring food to the villagers in their homes in the mountains while laying the groundwork for a local health system that could grow into the future. He planned for a holistic, long-range program.

In Addis Ababa, however, where we both were staying, Berggren was working fourteen-hour days establishing credibility with Ethiopian government staff, channeling medical and relief supplies that were flooding the airport of Addis Ababa to the project area, meeting leaders from Yfrat and Timuga. I needed to hear his plan, amorphous as it still was, in order to begin a training design. I could not even find time to have a meal with him, much less a briefing on the overall plan.

Wisely, I made no training design until I could find that time. I did no planning because I was not yet a definer of learning objectives. Until we had a clear conceptual framework for the skills, knowledge, and attitudes the staff needed to learn in order to do the job, I could not set up a program. As a wise man once said: "Don't just do something, sit there." I sat there. It was a great temptation to get started by designing a plan for training in the familiar modes of the agency's development programs. It was not easy to sit there, study Ethiopian history and read the literature to get some sense of the culture and the painful problem, and talk to old friends from Tanzania whom I found working in Addis Ababa. All around me swirled a frenzy of activity. I sat still, reading, observing, visiting, listening, waiting for time with the decision makers.

One Sunday afternoon the promised time arrived. I locked the door of my hotel room, sat down with the good doctor, and said: "Talk!" My questions followed a familiar pattern. We used the seven steps of design to get a comprehensive framework of his plan.

- *Who.* Who were the new staff to be? All the adult population of Yfrat and Timuga who could move to Addis had done so. Those who remained had been decimated by the drought. The only available recruits were youth from the towns along the main road that had a food supply line from Addis Ababa. These young people would be recent high school graduates with no English and no prospect of jobs except this one. They had no work experience. They had no health-related skills. They felt themselves, as townsfolk, a class above the peasant population they would be serving. They would be strangers to the mountain villages where they would be working.

- *Why.* The present situation (*why*) was the drought, of course, which called for relief operations at intense levels and teams of skilled workers to manage a relief and development program that was in the making. How could I come to understand the doctor's complete vision of this holistic program clearly enough to share it with the youth? They had to be made to see that this was not merely a relief operation but a process toward ongoing development systems. The projected outcome was their ability to manage all the tasks in such a development program.

The goals of the relief and development program were, first, to get food to the people so that they did not have to leave their homes. Second, staff were to establish systems for agriculture, health, and transportation from those villages—systems that could lead to social and political strength in the near future. Drought was not a stranger to these folks. They needed their local systems strengthened so that they could handle years of drought and times of ample harvests. The training would have to make this clear to the community. What would we teach in the short time available? This, in fact, was what had to be determined soon.

The Learners

It was a cold afternoon in Epheson. The chairman of the village stood and interviewed the gathered group of sixteen young men and women. The girls were shy and quiet, the boys clearly desperate for the job. Since we had no other source of supply for our staff, their concern was unnecessary. But they knew no English! How in the world could we create a dialogue with them? How could I teach them what they needed to know to do the job? Into the midst of this shy and gangly group of young people strode the answer to my questions: Fatuma, a mature, lean Afar nomad, a leader of her tribe. She had asked the chairman if she could join the group in training so that she could assure her people that they, too, would be part of the relief and development program. The Afar lived in tents in the mountains and herded camels. They and their herds were dying of the drought and desperately needed this relief program.

The chairman looked questioningly at us. Would I accept Fatuma into the group? She could not speak Amharic or English. She was old enough to be the mother of the young men and women standing around waiting to be hired. She stood there, tall and sure, with her rifle on her shoulder, smiling hopefully at me and at the men who would make this life-and-death decision. "I want her!" I smiled back at Fatuma and began a profound but wordless friendship.

I speak no Afar. Fatuma speaks no English. But we have communicated deeply in all the years since that day. I knew intuitively that Fatuma, without words, could define learning needs for the group and for me.

Months later, after the training when I was leaving Ethiopia, Fatuma made a short speech in her native Afar tongue. It was translated for me into English: "When these troubles are over, I will invite you to our Afar camp in the mountains. I will kill a camel to celebrate your coming, and the young men and women of our tribe will dance for you!" We had begun a friendship on that cold December afternoon, a friendship that would lead to learning on all sides. Here is the key to adult learning. Without it there is no honest defining of learning needs, no dialogue, no listening: the key is the respectful relationship of learner and teacher. As we see in this instance, such a relationship does not even need a common language.

Quantum thinking shows us that everything is related and that a program is more than the sum of its parts. The decision I made that afternoon on a hillside in Epheson was good quantum thinking. I knew intuitively that Fatuma's perception of this program was important. We'll soon see how important it was.

The Program and the Process

The sixteen young men and women went home for their gear and settled into the Epheson hotel with Fatuma and me. The hotel ($1 a night and highly overpriced) provided a large room for the training. Nobody suspected that we did not yet have a training course. We had hired an Ethiopian civil servant from Addis Ababa to be translator. He knew English and some Afar. He was to work by my side for the three weeks of "training." The rest of the team from the United States was going back to Addis to continue organizing logistics for the start of the program in four weeks' time. I still did not know what they wanted these young people to know. Once again, I locked the doctor in our hotel room and threatened, begged, cajoled: "Look, you are the definer of the skills, knowledge, and attitudes these people need to run this program. You have to let me in on the big picture."

Berggren described his vision. In lieu of building a relief station, he hoped to build a transport system that could bring food to the abandoned villages, trusting that people would return home when they discovered there was food available there. (Mountain villagers in Ethiopia have an incredible "bamboo wireless" that did indeed get this information to families as far away as Addis Ababa.) Then they could nurse their children back to health, feeding them amply from the relief stores, plant when the rains came, and harvest in the new season. They could continue with their lives in their own homes. SCF would provide development services: health systems, seeds, agricultural education, water systems, all that could get them started again on a sound basis. The government would then take over these services as basic social infrastructure for this area.

The villages near Epheson in the mountains of Yfrat and Timuga were remote and virtually inaccessible. Rough roads could be built. (Indeed, these roads were completed by the very men who came back home to find food.) The sixteen young staff people would be expected to organize the villagers to receive food, distribute food, vaccinate the infants, give vitamin A to prevent blindness among infants, measure and weigh all children and document the information so that those at greatest risk could receive special care, enroll all families so that continued services could be ensured, identify the very sick and dying for emergency care and give that emergency care at an aid station, and explain the long-range program to mothers so they would bring the children for continued care and vaccinations. There we had it. At last the learning needs—the skills, knowledge, and attitudes these young people needed to do the job—had been defined by the program's directors. I gulped and asked: "What else do they need to learn in four weeks?"

Dr. Berggren and I drew great charts of protocols as they worked themselves out in the villages. A protocol, in this situation, was a system of related activities in a very strict sequence that got a job done with assured quality. These protocols related one to the other so that the whole program could be seen as a flow of activities. Berggren's definition of learning needs was straightforward and comprehensive: this was it! I could have at that moment turned his protocol into activities involving specific skills, knowledge, and attitudes and set up a program. The needs assessment, however, was not yet complete. What about the other definers? The program director would live with this program long after Berggren and I had left. What did he want? The political leaders had to know that they were in charge of what went on in their region. What did they want? How did these men define the learning needs of the group? What did Fatuma and the young men and women want from this training course and the program? My job was to fit all these needs together as the content of the training course.

One thing we decided early: all sixteen of the youth and Fatuma would know how to do all the tasks in the protocols. There would be no specialists on this small staff. I asked the program director to spend time with the political leaders, describing the protocols and the overall program, asking them their hopes for the training. He and I had some time together to review the curriculum. However, later developments would show it was not nearly enough for me to know his intentions. Perhaps we should have designed a system for continued input from the director's office on the training event. After all, he was their supervisor and would be responsible for the success of their work and that of the overall program. Here was a case where role clarification was inadequate. We were to suffer the consequences of this error.

We later recognized that in our haste we had left out a crucial element of this picture as definers of learning needs for the training: the parents themselves and the men and women of Yfrat and Timuga who would be served by this group of town youth. A challenging strategic question remains. How could I have gotten their opinion on this design?

Who Needs What as Defined by Whom?

This WWW question, from Thomas Hutchinson of the University of Massachusetts School of Education, Amherst (1978), proved a useful instrument in discovering the learning needs and resources of the group. I discovered that such a question is never definitively answered. It must be asked again and again. New situations, new complexities, arise to change the *who* and the *what* and even the definers, the *whom*.

Who would teach this course? I might design it, but I surely could not teach them to give vaccinations or do emergency aid. We could get the local government doctor in Epheson to do that. I could teach most of the other items on the protocols with the help of our translator and, as it proved, my friend Fatuma. We started on a Monday morning in December. The young people were anxious to make good, since this was the only job in town. The translator was apprehensive. Fatuma sat proudly at a table by herself. I felt very much alone in the mountains of northern Ethiopia, immensely frightened by the prospect ahead of me. These young people and Fatuma had to be ready to begin the relief program when the program director arrived with the first shipments of relief food early in January. Over four hundred thousand men, women, and children waited upon the success of this program. Their lives depended on it. This was an educational challenge to match all others.

As a learning task for us all, I invited the group to draw a large wall map of the area, putting in all the vital information they thought I should know. I learned that the young people did know a great deal about the people of the town of Epheson but less about those in the mountain villages. Fatuma, of course, knew her people well. I learned that we had two artists in the group. I watched them all work together and saw that the boys continually took over from the girls yet were quick to defer to Fatuma. I watched who made decisions about what information should go on the rough map. This was all done in Amharic and Afar, words translated into English here and there, with much laughter and complete chaos throughout the design of the strategic map that emerged. We used that map constantly during the course, adjusting it to reality as we learned more.

The dialogue had begun. The initial problem was my education, not theirs. This was a shock to them, I could see. This was not like any school they had ever been to before. I asked each person to cite the most important item on the wall map for them. As their replies were translated, and I documented them, I learned a bit about each person's value system. I could see that this needs assessment was going to be an ongoing process. From among the natural friends who had been visible in the drawing of the map, we set up learning teams for accountability. The teams were mixed: men and women. Two of the young men knew some Afar, as I had noticed, so they were able to work in a team with Fatuma. Nothing would be so useful in this training program as their working in teams, preparing them to work in teams in the field, making it safe for them to make mistakes, question, and be unsure, and creating a quality-control group of peers. Competition among these teams was soon evident— not a destructive competition but a natural *com + petition*, asking together how the job could be done well, done better (*com*: with, *petition*: asking). Lavish affirmation, a central factor in this dialogue approach, was soon working, even through translation, to get these young people and Fatuma to relax into the job. I discovered that these sixteen youth were literate and numerate, knew Ethiopian history, and felt deeply about the drought and the need for their country to become self-reliant. They understood that the ravaging of trees from the mountains to provide firewood and charcoal for the growing urban population had been a major cause of this drought. They evidenced little knowledge of the sociopolitical forces involved in this geophysical catastrophe. Since they were semi-urban youth from towns along a main road, they had much to learn from rural Ethiopians. The culture of the roadside is not the culture of the mountainside, as they were soon to discover.

Imagine what would have happened if I had asked this group directly, through the translator, what they thought they needed to learn. Such an approach to needs assessment would have resulted in nothing authentic or useful. The design of the wall map, the open questions, and the dialogue among the participants were spontaneous and natural. Even if I could not understand the words, I knew they were naming real needs, vital issues, important factors in this complex program. They felt safe in the learning environment. I had prepared large charts of the overall program as we envisioned it; the protocol steps were dramatically drawn via stick figures. After going through the entire scenario through translation step by step, I asked them to come up in teams of twos and write the Amharic words that described each step. The charts became a bright mass of Cyrillic characters, and the teams argued loudly over what had been written. Again I was on the outside, looking in, while they defined their job descriptions. They felt safe to disagree with one another. In time, they would feel safe to disagree with me and with the program director. I have found that the moment of dissent in a course is a rich moment of learning for all. Modeling a true attitude of inquiry and learning is perhaps the most useful thing a teacher of adults can do. This principle uses the quantum concept of uncertainty and celebrates duality or "both/and" thinking, energy, and participation.

I had to trust what the translator said. We moved very slowly, of course. I had to read more of the physical language—the gestures, the questions on foreheads and faces—in this training event than ever I had before. *Who needs what as defined by whom?* This useful question enabled me to compare their perception of learning needs with the perceptions of other definers. The chairman and other political officers in Epheson had a learning agenda that was not at all surprising: they wanted the group to learn how to use and strengthen the political units in the mountains and bring the political message of the party to the villagers. I had to accept their agenda. It was my job to incorporate it somehow into the overall set of objectives of the training.

The achievement based objectives we set were in fact achieved by the end of the three weeks through the learning tasks set up for their training. When senior staff arrived in January, we demonstrated their skills and knowledge by doing all the protocols in sequence on the large field outside the classroom. It was clear they were accountable for all the skills, knowledge, and attitudes taught in the training. How did they know they knew? They did it.

Teamwork

These young people had come from a school system that apparently had never used teamwork in learning. Yet Fatuma had no trouble working on a team, since that was how her Afar people always worked. The small-group work was, as noted earlier, vital in the practice of collaboration and mutual help. We had an amusing but significant event during the training, which I describe here to show how leadership within a group emerges if you are in real dialogue with the people involved. This story also demonstrates two quantum principles: relatedness and participation.

One morning I arrived to start off a series of learning tasks only to discover that the teams had become twos. The love bug had bitten. We now had eight pairs of adolescents looking lovingly at one another, not at all part of their teams or the project! It was a scene from a high school classroom. What to do? I did not understand this culture, but I knew I needed their attention for the work at hand. I had to address this problem. The translator looked appealingly to me, indicating that he had no idea what to do. I had to admit defeat. I stopped the task and stood silently for a moment to catch their eye. Then I said to the translator: "Please tell the group I am going outside. I will be waiting there until they are ready to get to work. If they are not ready to work, I will get into the Land Rover and drive to Addis Ababa, where I will call the director and tell them the program cannot continue."

As I walked around outside the hotel, I could feel my legs buckle. Was this culturally appropriate? Would they call my bluff? How could I call off a multimillion dollar program, with half a million people's lives at stake, because of a training problem? I thought of the principle of immediacy. These young people were having a severe test of the immediacy of their commitment to this job.

After a very long ten minutes, the translator called me in. There on the front table was Fatuma's rifle. In the room, I found an air of quiet expectancy and rapt attention. I went on setting the task of the day, smiling at Fatuma, who sat innocently in the back row. There was no other evidence of the outbreak of seriousness in the room, but her rifle lay on that front table every day. How she had communicated across cultures, across languages, across generations to those young people is still a mystery. She did it, however, and I learned that I was not the only teacher in that room.

This incident was also part of the needs assessment. The young people manifested their need for intimacy; I made my own needs very clear; Fatuma showed her need and capacity for leadership. In doing a needs assessment, one must constantly listen to diverse and sometimes conflicting statements of the needs being met by a program. The seven steps of design focus on the learning needs of the learners themselves in the light of the potential impact of a program on the community or organization.

Quantum theory, with its reliance on the intrinsic chaotic order of nature, now offers me a sense that our program decisions, informed as well as can be by our needs assessment, will be beneficial. We cannot fail to do a learning needs and resources assessment; we also cannot do a perfect needs assessment. Let the dialogue begin before the course does, and know that learners will be encouraged by your intentional listening to them.

Design Challenges

- In any educational program you are designing, how do you discover the learning needs of the participants? How can the WWW question help you: *Who needs what as defined by whom?* Who are some of the definers of learning needs in your situation?

- What difference would it make to you, as a student in an educational program, to be invited by the professor to share your perception of your own learning needs?

How would it make that program more immediate for you if you could do so?

- What are some innovative ways you have used to do a learning needs and resources assessment? How have you tried to be inclusive?

- In the Appendix there are a number of suggestions for ways to do a learning needs and resources assessment. Which of them looks useful to you?

5

Safety

Creating a Safe Environment for Learning

You read in Chapter One about the principle of safety that guides the teacher throughout planning, learning needs and resources assessment, and first moments of the course. You saw the results of a safe learning environment in the Ethiopia case. Safety enables the teacher to create an inviting setting for adult learners. Adults have shown that they are not only willing but also ready and eager to learn when they feel safe in the learning environment. Trust in the competence of the design and the skills of the teacher enables learners to feel safe. Trust in the feasibility of the objectives and the relevance of these objectives also makes them feel safe. Allowing small groups to find their voices enhances the power of safety. Trust in the sequence of activities builds safety. Realization that the environment is nonjudgmental ensures safety. In the following story of a community education program in Tanzania, watch how safety was sadly eroded for all the learners in the program.

The principle of safety works for learners and teachers alike in an adult learning situation. There have been countless programs of community education aimed at development in Third World nations such as Tanzania. Many such programs, despite significant investments of funds, personnel, and time, never achieve the goals stated with such assurance in the proposals. What are some of the causes of recurrent failure? Political issues, economic structures, cultural customs, history, deep-seated prejudice, and racism—these are some of the factors involved.

This story tells of one of those small, failed programs and reviews the failure in the light of principles of dialogue education. We examine one community education program in Musoma near Lake Victoria and the role of one of the principals, Auni Makame. We will try to see how the absence of safety added this community education program to the pile of development failures.

The Problem and the Setting

Tanzania, listed by the United Nations as one of the poorest nations in the world, is engaged in a constant struggle for survival in the global economy as well as for development. It is estimated that it would take fifty years for a Tanzanian farmer to earn what a poverty-level family earns in one year in the United States. The great majority of the thirty million people of Tanzania live in rural areas. Peasant farmers in the rural villages face the formidable tasks of development: building durable homes, constructing latrines, providing a supply of clean water, raising sufficient food for their families, building schools and clinics, raising cash crops to provide some income, building linkage roads to main arteries. Villagers need education in technical skills for improved agriculture and small enterprise and in community organizing.

The Learners

After having studied with Anne Hope and Sally Timmel of the Training for Transformation program in Kenya, my colleague and I designed a proposal for funds for a program we entitled Community Education for Development (CED). We intended to do training using Paulo Freire's dialogue approach with local Catholic church leaders in the district of Musoma. We were generously funded by a German Catholic development foundation, Misereor.

Our small education project was an extension arm of the Makoko Family Center in Musoma, which offered a three-week intensive residential course to families in faith and child care, health, homemaking, agriculture, animal husbandry, and politics. Some families returned for further courses of stage 2 and stage 3 of this integrated development program. All returned to their own village farms after stage 1 with some new skills and ideas. The center had been urged by funding groups to develop an extension program, since there was not any follow-up program or structural support for these families to effect permanent change in their own lives or in their villages. These were the "leaders" we would gather, in their villages, for continuing training in management, communication, and leadership. Local Tanzanian government leaders were tolerant of the experiment, since it offered the kind of training needed by village leaders. These church folk were often leaders in their community and the village. We invited local government bureaucrats from the town of Musoma to attend our week-long programs in the neighboring villages and also invited the Catholic church pastors to attend.

Church authorities had given us permission to work in the diocese. They tolerated the idea of two women doing courses for Makoko Center families, catechists (local parish teachers of the catechism or manual of faith), and parish councils on invitation of the local parish priest. When the learning began to make itself felt in significant transfer—villagers showing new, responsible, and accountable attitudes—the churchmen began to show new interest.

Makame had heard of our program in his village on an island in Lake Victoria. He had founded this village with fishermen who had been coming to fish the lake from inland. Makame, himself a fisherman, had called together some of his friends and formed that village on a small island near Musoma. He later resigned as chairman of the village committee, but the fishermen still gratefully thought of him as their leader. Makame was a reputed Tanganyika African National Union (TANU) leader who proved to have good connections within that political party.

Makame had also started a small industry in Musoma: making chicken feed available to village families. Raising chickens was a viable household enterprise, but good chicken feed was very hard to come by. He had a small factory on the outskirts of town where he made a decent chicken feed out of an unlikely assortment of grains and animal waste. Makame was a local philosopher, inventor, and searcher. He had a high school education and was an avid reader. He made a living through the chicken feed factory for his wife and three young children, who lived in a small house in Musoma town. So Makame had the technical skills to teach what villagers needed. He had heard of our program from villagers who had done one of the short courses. He liked what he heard and came to visit us in our little house in Makoko. After introducing himself, he said, "I want to come to a course. I want to learn from you!" Makame felt safe enough to ask for what he saw he needed.

We were honored and delighted. We went to his island village and led a course with the village committee. He liked what he saw and told us that TANU in Musoma needed this participative, political, person-centered education in all the villages. He accompanied us into parish council leadership workshops for more courses, working with us in villages where Makoko families were the majority. It never occurred to us at the time that we were not providing any safety for Makame or the villagers. They liked him as a man and appreciated his input into the program, enhancing our Swahili and offering stories, images, proverbs, and metaphors from his family history and the political history of the country. However, Makame was a Muslim. And this program was the extension arm of the Makoko Christian Family Center.

The Program and the Process

CED had a six-member program committee formed of three parish priests, the priest who directed the Makoko Family Center, and the two of us. The three priests saw CED as a means to train catechists, those who taught newcomers the basics of the Catholic faith. The Makoko Family Center's director saw CED as a means to follow up the progress of the Makoko families. We two women educators on staff saw the program as broad development training that used Freire's approach with villagers toward their own personal and community development. As members of this program committee we never considered the obvious lack of safety among ourselves, did any serious reflection on the implications of the process being used, or worked on our own communication problems. We needed some quantum thinking about the whole!

The program committee itself needed a CED workshop in management, leadership, and communication skills. None of the priests on the committee ever attended a CED village course. Only one parish priest, who invited us to work with his parish council and catechists, attended the course. Therefore, these men did not know what we were doing and had never stayed long enough to find out.

Women in the Catholic Church had a very specific role at this time: teaching, nursing, cooking, supporting the priests in their efforts. Like faithful wives they were to be backstage, always there when needed, seen but not heard. The two of us in CED did not fit that mold. We did not know enough at the time about the principles of adult learning to provide for ourselves and all others the safety that would enable all of us to grow together. I did not know the quantum concept of participation: that people perceived the world from their own context. I did not comprehend that, in fact, all of us were perceiving different worlds.

The skepticism of the men increased when the program committee was presented with our proposal to hire Auni Makame, a Muslim, as an associate in the program. We explained how he would open the program up to many more villages and how he would be an excellent link to the leadership development efforts of TANU. He would not cost a penny, either, since we had arranged that he could be funded as a Canadian University Services Organization (CUSO) volunteer. This was the first time in history that CUSO had accepted a local Tanzanian as a volunteer. CUSO had also been an early fun-der of CED and of the Makoko Center.

What could we have done at that moment using the principle of safety to redeem this adult learning situation?

- We might have taken a long time to build a relation-ship between Makame and the bishop and the director and individual priests. Makame was seen as "their friend."

- We might have organized meetings among the TANU officials and Makame and the church leaders where TANU leaders could speak for themselves about their appreciation of the program.

- We might have organized meetings between Makoko Center families and Makame. He needed only the oc-casion to build trust with the groups. They would have created the safety we all needed had they had the time to get to know us and Makame.

- We might have organized opportunities to address parishes at Sunday services about the program. Since our efforts were planned with individual parish priests who did not perceive our effort as an official diocesan program, we did not use the institution to make it safe for them to welcome us. We did not go to each parish council meeting, each church on Sunday morning, or to the diocesan council. We did not feel safe, as women in an experimental venture, and we projected that feel-ing onto the program. The quantum principle of partic-ipation would have helped us understand the thinking of the priests. What they perceived was their reality.

- We might have taken time in preparation with the pro-gram committee to do strategic planning for CED by asking: Who are the stakeholders in this program?

What is our collective vision? What is our mandate? What actions should we undertake? Holistic quantum thinking would have helped here.

Simon Blackburn in his book *Think* (2000) says: "How we think about what we are doing affects how we do it or whether we do it or not." We simply did not know the theory we needed at the time to honor the context and create safety by optimal participation.

The Swahili proverb tells it all: *Kupotea njia ndiko kujua njia!* "By losing the way one learns the way!" We have learned from this experience that the safety of the program organizers and teachers is as important as that of the learners. We now insist that organizations who contract for training make sure that their senior managers take full part in the programs.

Finally, after much negotiation, Makame was accepted on staff. It was assured that he would not cost the diocese any money and that he would work under close supervision. Makame had a motorcycle provided by CUSO for all its volunteers; my colleague and I had small motorbikes, and together the three of us would roar along the dirt paths into a sleepy village to wake the residents to workshops on new ways of communicating, managing, and working together. The two of us, American women, were grateful to have a Tanzanian on board at last. Perhaps he could guide us in ways of teaching that would be more culturally appropriate to rural village life. Among the three of us there was safety and an exciting mutual learning dynamic.

Six Considerations

From long experience teaching in Tanzania before this program, I had learned that effective adult learning and teaching is

- Political—that is, it has to do with power and the distribution of power both in the process and in the content selected.

- Problem posing—that is, it is a dialogue around topical adult themes with adult materials evoking affective, psychomotor, and cognitive responses. From a quantum perspective, today I would say "examining potential" rather than problem posing.

- Part of a whole—that is, it must have follow-up and continuity. In quantum terms, this aspect considers the whole context of the learners' situation.

- Participative—that is, everyone involved will have time to speak, listen, and be actively engaged in the learning. In quantum terms, they construct their new skills, concepts, and attitudes to fit their context.

- Person-centered—that is, its purpose is the development of all the people involved. The purpose is not merely sharing information.

- Prepared—that is, from the initial learning needs and resources assessment to the use of the seven steps of design to the design of materials, the learning is prepared for a particular group of learners and adequate time is used to make it ready.

I included these six considerations in my research for my doctoral dissertation at University of Massachusetts (Vella, 1978). In Tanzania at the time we were building a body of theory together as we documented and reviewed the processes and products of the community education program. I believe we three were the chief learners in this adult education program.

Community Theme: Listening to One Another

Despite the serious problems in the program's design, we had some wonderful experiences in villages and parishes. Rural folk were hungry for the chance to tell their stories and share their feelings about local issues. They wanted to know how to be honest neighbors, how to manage small projects effectively to bring in needed money and resources, how to communicate better among themselves. There was safety enough in some situations for people to be very honest indeed.

When asked what they most wanted to learn, villagers invariably replied "kusikilizana." This Swahili word means to hear one another. Most of these villagers were preliterate. If they were in their thirties or forties, they had not had occasion to go to primary school in their village. We could not use charts with Swahili words on them, so we used many large line or stick drawings or found objects or representative colors. Village leaders had a great sense of the symbolic and could immediately relate to selecting a piece of colored cloth that represented the economic state of their village. "Green and red: there is a new harvest coming, showing green, but we don't know how much we will get at the market for it, so I also choose red for my anger at the low prices!" "Brown for the soil: we are farmers with our fingers in the earth." They clearly felt safe in speaking their minds and hearts to one another.

Listening to the themes of a community in a listening survey by living there and being with the people demanded more Swahili skills than we two Americans possessed. In the villages where he was accepted Makame could listen and reflect back to the people and to us what he had heard. In other villages, his being a Muslim made it unsafe for him to be present in the community. Some of the parish leaders went to the bishop to complain that a Muslim was coming to teach them. We soon discovered how uncomfortable it is not to have the safety needed for learners to learn or teachers to teach.

In one village in Musoma where we had been invited to teach the local leaders communications and management skills, we discovered an appalling polarization between the men and women. Men simply had no time for the women leaders, who had been elected by their peers. The men refused to listen to women when they spoke during the course. When women's groups made their reports, the men would talk to one another. One old man in particular, Amos, was impatient with our approach when we insisted on their listening more carefully to the women members.

"Let us get on with the seminar," he said at one point. "She is just wasting our time. After all, she is only a woman." These same men could speak very warmly about democracy and equality as political party leaders and Christian teachers. Apparently they were not aware of the incongruity of their attitude toward their mothers, wives, and daughters.

If we had been using monologue, we would have given them a stirring lecture in carefully chosen language about *ujamaa,* the national theme of familyhood and respect for all. We would have invited their questions and gone home feeling justified in the quality of our teaching. We were trying to use dialogue, however, and all the principles and practices of adult learning that were emerging from our work. So we took a chance by using a simulated situation to catch the attention of men and women alike. I felt entirely safe doing this simple drama, trusting the Tanzanian women to come up with some way to save the situation.

The simulation began when my colleague, as planned, entered the round, thatched hut where the village course was being held. She was rather agitated and asked to meet all the women in the middle of the room. The men sat quietly around the walls, wondering. The teacher explained, in a concerned voice, that a child of the village had fallen into a large pit and it was impossible to get him out. He was a tiny lad of four and was terrified in the dark hole. What could be done? Outside we could hear the distant wailing of a child: Makame was providing sound effects.

The first response from the women was: "Let us call the men!" "No use!" replied the teacher. "All of the men have gone into town to watch a football game. There are no men in the village at this time." "Then let us go and call them from town!" "No, there is not enough time. The child is very frightened. We have to do something immediately." Makame, outside, wailed louder. The village women entered the role play with great gusto, making various suggestions, almost all of them indicating their dependency on the men. The village men sat by and chuckled in delight at the drama. "We can find a ladder at the carpenter's shop." The wailing continued. "We can search for a long rope! The fishermen have one!" "We can go to the next village and call their men!" Then one of the women, in a very small voice, said: "We could use our kangas (shawls) and make a rope!" "Yes, we could tie all of our kangas together and make a rope long enough to pull him out of the pit!" More wailing!

With great glee, the village women whipped off their individual shawls, made of sturdy cotton, and began with feverish haste to tie them together, forming a long rope that was thrown out the door of the hut. A great cheer arose, from men and women alike in the hut, when we pulled in the frightened, lost child (a smiling, silent Makame).

In immediate reflection upon the activity, as the women laughingly recovered their kangas, we began with an open question: "What happened here?" One woman responded: "We discovered a way for ourselves, without the men! We used our own resources! We made it work! We worked together!" Then the teacher asked: "Whose idea was it to use the kangas?" One woman replied: "It was Maria's idea, but she had only one kanga!"

The next morning, old Amos came to me grumbling: "You! Last night, I could not sleep thinking of those women and their kangas!" The women had taught the men something very important, and they had taught themselves something even more important. Our job was to design and present the task, the simulation, in a safe, structured environment and invite their wise response. The environment of safety in that hut evoked their spontaneous creativity, collaboration, and communication.

Evaluation

Months afterward I happened to visit that village, and the women, seeing me, called out laughing, "We remember the kangas!" The safety we felt in that community had permitted us to deal with a sensitive problem through that simulation. There was no immediate indication of change in the men's relation to the women. This problem was so deep-seated in the culture that we and our CED program could do nothing further about it. But the women had made a safe beginning. One old man's sleep was disturbed by this new concept. That might be the only possible indicator of success.

Ultimately, the suspicions that billowed around Makame made it impossible for him to continue working with us. His two-year contract with CUSO was continued through other development enterprises. The political, economic, cultural, and historical forces in that Christian community never really made it safe enough to include him in the program. We learned a hard lesson about program development: community organizing, assiduous preparation, personal contacts with key individuals and groups in a community are all necessary to establish a safe environment for community education. Even then, the issues facing a community often have such deep cultural roots that building awareness on certain issues may be unacceptable or unsafe.

Perhaps adult learning is always dangerous. A fifty-year-old woman in one of our programs in North Carolina, investigating a welcoming undergraduate program for women at a small southern college, told the admissions officer: "My husband says he is glad for me to go back to school, as long as I do not change!" It was not safe for the husband to have his wife in college. As I look back on this Tanzanian program, I think of Donald Oliver's brilliant distinction between technical and ontological knowledge: "Technical knowledge refers to adaptive, publicly transferable information or skills; ontological knowing refers to a more diffuse apprehension of reality, in the nature of liturgical or artistic engagement. In this latter sense, we come to know with our whole body, as it participates in the creation of significant new occasions—occasions which move from imagination and intention to critical self-definition to satisfaction and finally to perishing and new being" (1989, p. 63).

Do you hear the quantum themes in Oliver's statement? I am aware that in our small, precarious community education program in Musoma, Tanzania, we were dealing almost all the time with problems of ontological knowing. I have learned much from that experience but mostly that safety in the learning situation, for teacher and learner, is even more necessary when we are facing the complex challenges involved in advancing learning in a cross-cultural situation.

Today in Tanzania, Benjamin Mkapa, the president, has taken on the challenge of dealing directly with "corruption and sleaze among leaders" (http:www.Tanzania). Community education for development is still called for in that struggling nation. Safety is a global concept. In the macro-economic environment of globalization, Julius Nyerere's description is important: "Globalization is like a boxing match, where a huge professional boxer faces a small amateur, and the umpire disappears." How can education and economics build safety into the picture of global development? This question is even more vital in today's world.

Design Challenges

- In your own teaching and learning situations with adults or others, how do you see safety as a variable you can control and assure? What can you do to make sure it is available to you as teacher and to the learners?

- What do you discern in this story as our worst move? That is, what seemed to lead most directly to a loss of safety and the loss of Makame's services in the development education program?

- Why do you think the Swahili proverb—*Kupotea njia ndiko kujua njia!* "By losing the way one learns the way!"—is relevant here?

6

Sound Relationships

Using the Power of Friendship

This chapter examines a situation where the relationship between the instructor and the learner was clearly an important factor in the learning process. I call this principle sound relationship—which implies that there is friendship but no dependency, fun without trivializing learning, dialogue between adult men and women who feel themselves peers. It has roots in quantum theory. Listen to Margaret Wheatley: "In the quantum world, relationship is the key determiner of everything. Subatomic particles come into form and are observed only as they are in relationship to something else. They do not exist as independent 'things.' Quantum physics paints a strange yet enticing view of a world that, as Heisenberg describes it, 'appears as a complicated tissue of events in which connections of different kinds alternate or overlap or combine and thereby determine the texture of the whole' (1958, p. 107.) These unseen connections between what were previously thought to be separate entities are the fundamental ingredient of all creation" (Wheatley, 1999, p. 11).

In Chapter One you examined the power of sound relationships in enhancing adults' potential for learning. Sound relationships for learning involve respect, safety, open communication, listening, and humility. The quantum concepts of energy and the relatedness of all things are at work here. Learners' energy is much more available when they trust their teacher and are trusted in a learning situation.

The Situation and the Setting

The power relationship that often exists between a "professor" and learners is a function of a system where power is often used to dominate. Our efforts through education to build a world of equity and mutual responsibility cannot be designed without attention to the power of sound relationships. If I, as adult educator, show myself accessible to learners through an early dialogue with a learning needs and resources assessment and respond to learners' questions with respect and affirmation in a safe environment, that world of equity already exists. The quality of the relationship between teacher and adult learner is the central principle in this story.

I went to Indonesia to do a two-week training of Save the Children staff on the island of Java. The training was difficult. It was a large group, and all learning tasks had to be translated into Bahasa Indonesian and then the responses translated back into English. Many organizational issues arose. But the end result was quite rewarding.

One of the Indonesian staff, a gifted artist and physician, put the concepts and principles of popular education into symbolic paintings of Indonesian metaphors that represented each of the ideas being taught. That artist, Margie Ahnan, two years later found herself in the United States at a large school of public health, somewhat frustrated by the academic rendering of community health education. Her advisor at the university mentioned that there was one person in the United States whom Dr. Ahnan should meet: Jane Vella of Jubilee Popular Education Center in Raleigh, North Carolina. She was amazed at the synchronicity of the reference and called me at once.

Jubilee had a fellowship program that invited international students of community education to come to Raleigh to work closely with us for three months. I invited Dr. Ahnan to take this fellowship. She accepted with alacrity and soon arrived in Raleigh.

How does one organize a three-month program for an Indonesian medical doctor so that she can go back to Indonesia and teach other health professionals how to use these principles and practices? What are the operative principles in such a situation? Quantum theory suggests that relationship is vital. Could the operative principle be that simple: a developing friendship between adult learner and adult teacher?

The Program and the Process

Our one great advantage was the informality of the situation. We set the boundaries. Dr. Ahnan had just come from two years of a graduate school program that she had found somewhat disappointing. She is a brilliant woman, an experienced physician, and a gifted artist. We sat together to design our program from the draft I presented. I showed her the Jubilee calendar of training and educational events that she would attend during the three-month fellowship. I told her that I hoped she would enhance each event. She was excited at the immediacy of engagement in community education in North Carolina.

After offering her a long reading list and suggesting that she select a book she wanted to start with, we set up a daily seminar to have a dialogue about her reading and anything else she was learning. I was, during these seminars, to learn a great deal about the Indonesian perspective. Had I the advantage of my present understanding of quantum theory, I would have celebrated even more the advantage of interpreting classic adult learning theory in a new context. I was not the "professor" during these dialogues. The authors of the books were doing the teaching, and we were examining together the significance of what they had to offer in the light of our distinct experiences and contexts. It was a rich learning time for both of us. The quantum concept of participation was at work. "We have all learned from experience that solutions don't transfer. These failures (of cross-cultural consultations) have been explained by quantum physics. In a quantum world, everything depends on context, on the unique relationships available at the moment. Since relationships are different from place to place and moment to moment, why would we expect that solutions developed in one context would work the same in another?" (Wheatley, 1999, p. 173)

After the first week, the role distinction of teacher-student began to dissolve. We were friends learning together. There was a distinct generation gap, of course. I was old enough to be her grandmother. But there was no gap in the acceptance of the learning potential of this experience for both of us. As Freire reminds us: "Only the student can name the moment of the death of the professor." I would add: And only the professor can welcome that moment!

In our developing relationship as friends, we were able to examine each situation in the program with openness and struggle with our different perspectives without guilt or shame. Every educational program is a new context with new and challenging relationships. I think of the power of the Sufi proverb quoted by Wheatley (1999, p. 10): "You think because you understand one you must understand two, since one and one makes two. But you must also understand *and*."

As we made and remade her program, we discovered our own value systems anew. I did not agree with many of Dr. Ahnan's perspectives on women's roles, task allotment, or the use of class distinctions. She did not agree with many of my perspectives on task priority, egalitarian relationships, or the teacher's role. In the struggle, we both learned. We so honored one another that it was necessary to celebrate the opposites we represented. Quantum duality was the accepted backdrop of our dialogue.

The relaxed atmosphere during the three months of her fellowship was a vital part of the design—much laughter and great tennis and long, leisurely meals with conversation that went late into the night. We welcomed friends who came often to meet this exciting Jubilee Fellow from Indonesia and share in the learning and teaching. Our relationship enabled Dr. Ahnan to learn; it also helped her to teach and get feedback so that her learning could be transferred later to her own cultural setting. She did not have to abandon her

Indonesian perspective. She did not have to fit into an acceptable pattern or keep quiet when she heard something she disagreed with. The advantages of a one-on-one mentoring situation like this are many. There is immediacy: questions are answered or issues confronted as they arise. There is complete engagement: the program is designed to meet the learning needs of one person. Most of all there is time: the person not only spends time alone but also has full access to the mentor. There is the opportunity for disagreement in a friendly relationship that invites honest opposition. We saw how right the poet William Blake was when he said: "Opposition is true friendship." In such a relationship we could address errors in judgment and logic, challenge incomplete thinking, and defend and celebrate cultural distinctions.

This experience for Dr. Ahnan was such a far cry from her recent graduate school program that she challenged me to test ways to introduce these variables into the formal school setting. The principle is this: a sound relationship between mentor and adult learner is productive of learning. Within that relationship, the variables we can control are time, affirmation, mutual respect, open dialogue, open questions that invite dialogue, engagement in significant work, role clarification, responsibility, and immediate response to questions and issues that are raised.

The one-on-one Jubilee Fellowship arrangement is one approach to getting all these variables into action. How can we structure a classroom, workshop, orientation, or training to bring all these variables into play? We know they work. How can we design our adult learning events so they work for larger groups of learners? Here are some practical suggestions for getting this relationship to work.

Time

Time is paramount. In a graduate course at the University of North Carolina School of Public Health, I arrange to be present one hour before class to meet one or more of the graduate students for reflection or response to questions. I invite them to call me whenever they are stuck in their research or design work. I tell them: "Don't stay stuck!" I schedule potluck dinners and picnics so we have leisurely time to talk. In a workshop, I schedule lunches and dinners with people so we can develop a relationship for future mutual support. In an orientation program in industry, we set up pairs of new workers and workers with experience who mentor one another through the program.

Mutual Mentoring

A hospice director in North Carolina, with over fifty people on staff, has devised a support system that enables relationships for learning and development to grow. Every three months, they set up pairs which are the mutual support teams for the next three months. What they do and how they do their mutual mentoring is entirely up to them. Their only charge is to "take care of one another." The relationships that develop as nurses care for secretaries, doctors care for nurses, technicians take the executive director to lunch when she is feeling down are amazing representations of the power of ʻ human beings to care when the scale is human and the structure is safe. This caring takes time. We have to be as creative as this director was in finding ways to structure time for mutual mentoring when we are dealing with large groups of learners. This creativity is part of our task as teachers of adults.

Lavish Affirmation

Affirmation is possible and necessary at every step of the way, whether with large numbers of learners or with small groups. Here the issue is not time or scale. It is your willingness as "professor" to affirm at every level, celebrate learning when you see it happening, and say, "Well done!" We can structure affirmation into a program by using open questions for constant feedback all the time: What did you find most useful in this session? Why? What would you suggest we change? Why? Such a design assumes there is something to celebrate and something to improve in any human endeavor. Instead of marking what is wrong on a paper or pointing out flaws in a performance, we begin by naming what went well. This is an attitude that must be taught to teachers of adults and practiced by them. I find that men and women who have the most trouble with offering affirmation feel most uneasy receiving it. Self-doubt projects. However, so does self-affirmation!

What about behavior or opinions that are counter to one's own value system? How does one affirm another when this occurs? I can always find it within me to say: "I honor the fact that you felt comfortable enough to say what you just said. I celebrate your strength. I do not agree with what you say and would love to argue with you about it." Affirmation is not always affirmation of the idea or opinion. It is always affirmation of the person. The end of affirmation is to have the person learn and develop. We can never control what another person thinks. We can nurture their thinking power by affirmation and build a learning relationship. Quantum theory teaches that other people are in relationship with us—it is up to us to determine what kind of a relationship it is.

Walter Wink in his classic text *Engaging the Powers* (1992) offers a compelling distinction between relationships that dominate and those that nurture and free. We, as adult educators, are challenged to examine our relationships with students, recognizing the subtle layers of social, economic, gender, and cultural factors, and work to make them as freeing as possible.

Tone of Mutual Respect

Mutual respect can best be structured by avoiding activities that deny it: gossiping, judging, committing "plops" (failing to acknowledge a statement or response), misrepresenting what another has said. Such respect is often a question of tone, as well. In the diverse cultural settings in which I have found myself, I learned early on that tone carries meaning. Simple courtesies of language "Please," "Thank you," "If you will . . ." carry all the more importance when they come from the "professor." Such humility, such gracious humanness speaks in any language and to any culture.

Carl Jung insisted that all those who wish to be clinical analysts (counselors) should themselves undertake a long, arduous program of analysis. Only such an experience would afford the mutuality he knew was necessary for a successful relationship between analyst and client. The same holds true in the adult learning process. We teachers have to honor our own need to learn. We must talk about that honestly. This is the greatest respect we can offer adult learners. *Respectare* is the Latin root of the word respect. It means "to see" *(spectare)* "again" *(re)*. I suggest it also implies "hearing again." Listening without interrupting is a simple structure for ensuring respect. We can do that even in large groups. Open dialogue can readily be structured in any event: teaching a complex concept, practicing a skill, or learning an attitude. Concepts can be presented as open systems—as the hypotheses they actually are—and the adult learner can be invited to examine, edit, and add to them from their experience and unique context and do something with them through learning tasks (Vella, 2000). Such a dialogue builds a relationship that inevitably leads to learning and development. Donald Oliver's distinction between technical and ontological knowing, mentioned in Chapter Five, can be "taught," for example, via open dialogue with adult learners organized in small task groups. The learning task for that could be

- Read this handout with the distinction between technical and ontological knowledge as described by Oliver.

- In pairs, name one learning experience when you felt what you learned was definitely technical knowing. Then name one event when you felt you were engaged in ontological knowing. We'll hear a sample of those different events.

In this learning task, the relationship for learning and develop-ment is not only between the teacher and the adult learner but, what is more significant, also within the learning pair. Dialogue, as I have said earlier, is among learners, of whom the teacher is one. When we look in Chapter Twelve at a new role for the professor, we will examine a common dilemma faced by teachers. What is the teacher's role while the adult learners are learning and developing through a well-designed learning task? This is where the poet John Keats's great concept of negative capability is helpful. Without the ability not to intrude but to wait, be patient, and be on call and ac-cessible as a resource, the teacher cannot be a catalyst for this qual-ity of learning. This is not an easy role. At one point in the fast-developing fellowship, Dr. Ahnan was designing charts, read-ing her books, preparing tasks for a design for an upcoming program, and writing her journal while I sat by somewhat bemused. I asked: "Just what's my role in all this?" She smiled: "Just be there, Jane, just be there!" That calls for negative capability and real humility.

My friend Robert Sigmon describes the response of his teacher to his request: "Teach me to pray." The teacher instructed him, "Sit still, keep quiet, pay attention." When I heard this I recognized the role of a learning teacher in dialogue education.

During a high-intensity graduate class at the School of Public Health, small groups were working industriously and somewhat noisily on a learning task. I sat in the corner of the room working just as industriously at my laptop computer, available to them, en-joying their energetic efforts. The department head looked in and asked me, "Why are they always so excited?" I replied confidently, "I think, Jim, it's because they are learning."

Another example of relationships in dialogue from that same graduate course comes from a day when a particular learning task took three hours. I sat in the same corner after telling the group I would visit task groups only on request, offer my response to their questions, and leave. At the end of three hours I had had one request, which took five minutes to deal with. I had to confess to the group that it was the hardest graduate class I had ever taught.

Negative capability is not easily learned. It is essential, however, in the development of sound relationships for learning. In a classroom the energy center is not only the professor, but also the learners.

Nonjudgmental Dialogue

Nonjudgmental dialogue is necessary for learning. The modeling of the professor can establish an ethical standard in the group that will prevail throughout the course. Judging stops spontaneity. We have good evidence of this from everyday life. In working with adult learners, who have often suffered from judgmental bosses, spouses, in-laws, ministers, sons, and daughters, the connotation of a judging remark is immense. The relationship between teacher and learners has to be built by avoiding judgment. When Dr. Ahnan made suggestions that were clearly based on an Indonesian perspective, I carefully affirmed her, argued with her opinion if need be, and tried very hard not to judge those opinions as right or wrong, good or bad. What, after all, did I know about Indonesian culture or the context of her work in the teeming city of Jakarta? How could I judge her design decisions for that unique situation? Here again is a call for negative capability—simply avoiding judging, waiting for more information, listening. I have observed: we teach the way we were taught. We also judge the way we are judged. The only way to break the cycle is through the practice of nonjudgmental dialogue, arguing with affirmation. We can structure it into our teaching and learning designs and, more important, model it in our relationships. This is quantum thinking at its best, honoring the centrality of context and the uniqueness of individual participation from the perspective of each individual's context.

Open Questions

Open questions that invite dialogue are a simple format for building confidence and creating a sound relationship for learning, developing, and listening. We understand the difference between a closed question, which calls for a yes or no reply or a single-word response, and an open question, which invites dialogue. The learning tasks set earlier in relation to the concepts of technical and ontological knowing were open questions: "In pairs, name one learning experience when you felt what you learned was definitely technical knowing. Then name one event when you felt you were engaged in ontological knowing." An open question invites reflection, consideration of cultural, gender, age, and personal values and awareness of implications. In practicing a computer skill: "What do you think might happen if you deleted a paragraph before saving it? What might it mean for your work?" In learning an attitude: "Suppose you were a young lawyer and you had the chance to clerk with Thurgood Marshall in the Supreme Court. Your parents were hostile to African Americans. So you turned down the chance. How would you feel today?"

It takes time and effort for an educator of adults to design appropriate and provocative open questions in order to invite significant dialogue. Many of us grew up in mechanistic systems where closed questions were answered in the back of the book. Our personal response was not invited; neither was honest dialogue. Open questions are the single, sure practice that invites critical thinking and effective learning. Open questions invite me and the people I teach to listen to one another with mutual respect.

Listen to what Danah Zohar says about dialogue in relation to her understanding of quantum theory: "I want to describe dialogue as an important and very particular process of our thinking and a powerful means by which we can grow new neural connections. I think it is a quantum process, a means of doing and using quantum thinking" (Zohar, 1997, p. 136).

Engagement in Significant Work and Responsibility

Engagement in significant work and responsibility are, of course, practical manifestations of a trusting relationship. Engagement can be structured by designing an orientation, training program, course, or any learning event so that adult learners are doing something of meaning to them. Small groups can take on meaningful learning tasks that are of immediate usefulness and be mentors to one another in the learning and completion of that task. Kurt Lewin (1951) made it very clear in his research that learning took place only when learners were actively engaged.

When Dr. Ahnan was invited to design the charts for a Jubilee program, design a learning task and lead it with a group, or prepare an evaluation instrument and test it within a learning event, she was learning. The task itself was her teacher. The engagement was the way she learned—by doing it. What is our role when learners are engaged in significant work? Again with a strong dose of negative capability, our role is to be a resource, to set the task clearly without ambiguity, make sure there are adequate physical resources to do it successfully, and get out of the way. Such engagement is not examination. This is not an activity to test knowledge, skills, or attitudes. This is why I am specific about engagement in *significant* work. We build a strong relationship when the adult learners understand, by the structure of the design, that we expect them to do an important job well. We are there while they are doing it. We have structured it and set up the tasks they need to do, but we do not do it for them. We sit still, pay attention, and keep quiet.

Role Clarification

Role clarification is a key aspect of building a strong relationship. When adult learners, in a large group or a one-on-one situation, are clear about their role, the tasks they will have to achieve to fulfill that role, and the boundaries involved, they can get on with the learning. When there is any ambiguity about their role, tasks, or boundaries, you know you are in for trouble. With Dr. Ahnan, I made clear at the beginning of the Jubilee Fellowship that her role was that of student. It was a time-bound role and she had paid for the privilege of working at Jubilee as a fellow. She was the one who decided how she spent her time. But when she decided to take part in a program and agreed to design charts, make an evaluation instrument, or lead a session, she would be held responsible for doing that task well. We signed an agreement to that effect.

In terms of what she did and when she did it in the Jubilee Fellowship, Dr. Ahnan had the deliberative voice. As an adult learner in this fellowship program, she was the decision maker. I had a consultative voice and could make suggestions about her program. However, it was her program (Vella, 1995, p. 160). When she decided to take part in a Jubilee program for other learners, the roles reversed. I had the deliberative voice and she had a consultative one. This clarification kept us safely apart, so we were not in one another's way, and kept us working smoothly together. It made for assured accountability on both sides, as well. I was accountable to Dr. Ahnan—to make suggestions, to be a mentor. She was accountable to herself and to Jubilee when she decided to work in a program. As a Jubilee Fellow, she was not accountable to me except in basic human courtesies and as a guest in a strange culture. I was accountable to her. Here is another point of transformation of the paradigm in adult learning. In traditional educational programs, the master is in charge and the students are accountable to him. In this approach to adult learning, however, the roles are mutual. This mutuality makes all the difference. It is what Thomas Kuhn calls a "paradigm shift" (Kuhn, 1970) and is, in my experience, the genesis of healthy relationships for learning and development.

Immediate Response to Questions

Immediate response to questions that are raised is an aspect of that accountability. How can this occur when you are working with a large number of adults? We need to creatively design structures that make this happen. Immediacy has been proven to be one of the basic aspects of adult learning. When an issue is hot, it is hot. Waiting to deal with it later risks the loss of a learning moment. Here are some structures that have worked in large groups to honor immediacy:

- Set the norm that any question that arises has priority over the task at hand. This means that adult learners are invited to interrupt the learning task to ask their question or raise their burning issue. This is not often easy to accept, as it can look like the proverbial red herring. But in my experience, one adult's question is often the unasked question of the whole group. It is useful to refer such a question to the group by what I call a *bouncing question*. "Before I respond, what do you think of Mary's question?" This continues the vital peer learning while leaving time for you to respond in full. You as teacher are thus developing a relationship for learning among peers.

- Structured time can be set before and after a session so that immediate concerns can be dealt with in dialogue. Other structured time can be set when the teacher is accessible outside the class.

- Being accessible by phone or e-mail is another way to deal with immediate issues. The onus is on the teacher to respond as quickly as possible to a question. If the response is not immediate, learners will often not call again.

- I use e-mail to deal with issues of feedback when clients or students are designing programs. We need not talk at all. They send me their draft designs or papers or whatever, and I make my notes on the draft and simply send it right back. This is a useful instrument for immediate response and feedback, confirming a relationship of mutual trust.

The Learning Moment

Capturing the learning moment is what all these structures aim at doing. We all have had the awesome experience of being present at a learning moment: the *aha!* moment when the concept is realized, when the abstract word becomes flesh! I know that moment by the quality of the silence that pervades the room, whether it is filled with a thousand, a hundred, ten adults, or just two of us. The quality of silence is a symbol of what Joseph Campbell (1972) calls a moment of "transparent transcendence." How many times in that Jubilee Fellowship did Dr. Ahnan and I enjoy that quality of silence as we sat together on the back porch? As a teacher in the formal school system for twenty years, I may have heard that powerful silence once or twice. Today, using this dialogue approach to adult learning, I hear such silence through these relationships once or twice daily.

Evaluation: Learning, Transfer, Impact

During the three-month fellowship, Dr. Ahnan demonstrated her learning in the designs she completed, the teaching she did in our programs, and her portfolio. From her position as a physician today in Indonesia, she tells me about her transfer of knowledge and skills to her workplace. She uses dialogue education in teaching public health nurses how to work with Indonesian women and their children. Her descriptive phrase for the results is a culturally apt metaphor: "These nurses are now sharing their own strengths, using all the principles and practices with the women. The tigers are loose in Java!" One can only imagine the impact.

Design Challenges

No matter what your engagement as an adult educator, administrator, designer of programs, teacher, or evaluator may be, the principle of respect and sound relationships can help.

- Consider one person with whom you have a constant interaction: a colleague, a peer, a secretary, a student, a boss. Take some time now to consider how you can de-sign a system to support a relationship for learning and development. Include all the aspects discussed in this chapter: time, mutual mentoring, affirmation, tone of mutual respect, nonjudgmental dialogue, open ques-tions that invite dialogue, engagement in significant work, responsibility, role clarification, immediate re-sponse to questions that are raised.

- What else would you add to this set of strategies from the perspective of your unique culture and personality? Your own cultural perspective and respect for your own context will offer you the most useful and successful strategies. Whatever the strategy, your unique personal style must be honored. The first sound relationship is with oneself.

7

Sequence and Reinforcement
Supporting Their Learning

You read in Chapter One about the important principles of sequence and reinforcement. *Sequence* means the programming of knowledge, skills, and attitudes in an order that goes from simple to complex and from group-supported to solo efforts, from smaller to larger tasks. Learning tasks can be readily examined for sequence. The manifestations in learners of a sense of safety, enthusiasm, and readiness to achieve indicate that sequence is being honored. When you, as teacher, see fear, confusion, or reluctance to try in the learner, it is time to test the sequence of the learning tasks. You may find you have not honored learners' need for small steps between tasks or their need for reinforcement.

Reinforcement means the repetition of facts, skills, and attitudes in diverse, engaging, and interesting ways until they are obviously learned. The design of tasks of reinforcement in adult learning is the job of the teacher. Although adult learners may do their own reinforcement through practical work and study, our accountable teaching designs must offer adequate reinforcement tasks to ensure learning.

Sequence and reinforcement are a set of principles that work remarkably well in the design of language learning and every other kind of teaching as well. A rare sequence of events led to a call from Dr. Tito Craige, an old friend. He asked if I would be willing to work with him to train young college students to teach Haitian migrant workers English through the Migrant and Seasonal Farm Workers organization (MSFW).

Dr. Craige and I were old friends from North Carolina State University, where he had burst into my office one morning to ask, "Are you Dr. Vella?"

"I am!"

"Well, you have the most interesting reserve shelf of books in the library!"

Craige had been browsing during a long day of research on his doctoral dissertation and had wandered over to the reserve shelves and seen my collection for my graduate course on adult education. Such a delightful and innovative meeting was only the beginning of even more delightful and fruitful encounters. I knew from experience that his telephone call offered great possibilities.

The Situation and the Setting

Craige described his dream to me. He had funds for a mobile classroom that would drive to migrant labor camps, equipped with all the materials and technology that would help workers learn what they needed to know. Teachers would teach them English, coping skills for entrance into a new society, how to get and keep a green card—in fact, all the skills, knowledge, and attitudes a migrant worker could use. He now had permission from growers to come into the camps. What he needed was a well-trained teacher corps, a group of skilled men and women familiar with the principles of adult learning, to do the job.

"Tito," I apologized, "I have never even been inside a migrant camp! I have never met a migrant worker! How in the world can I teach young people how to teach migrant workers? Here are my terms: I will spend this summer teaching in a migrant camp in your new program. This will provide me with the experiential base I need to speak with authority to the young people who want to be in this teacher corps."

The sequence here is vital: I could have designed a training course and then gone to the camps, or I could have designed and led a training course and then checked it out by observing the teachers at work in the camps. Intuitively, I was doing sound quantum thinking by respecting the unique situation that I knew I had to learn before designing a curriculum. I had to be there in this unique context before I taught others how to be there. Dr. Craige agreed with some reluctance, since he had wanted to do the training immediately. He set me up at a camp with a group of Haitian migrant workers whom I would teach literacy skills and English every Tuesday evening from 7 to 9. I attended the short MSFW orientation program for new teachers and set forth.

The Learners

I drove to McGee's Crossroads southeast of Raleigh, North Carolina, with some trepidation the first night. How would I present myself to these Haitian migrant workers? They had come to supplement the Mexican workforce and had to face not only a strange new world but also the antagonism of their fellow workers in the fields, mostly Hispanics, who naturally felt threatened by this new group. What would be the wisest first step for me to take? In the orientation we had heard all the history and legal aspects of the migrant situation. Yet it still was not clear to me. I knew these men were here without their families, whom they had left in Haiti. They had been hired for a single summer and were obliged to be back in Haiti by the end of the year. They would pick tobacco and vegetables in North Carolina through August and then follow the vegetable harvest stream up through Michigan before leaving in the fall.

Today, with a new awareness of a quantum world where the whole is seen as operative and more than the sum of its parts, I would want to know a great deal more about their homes and their hopes for the future. I knew I had to see them in their migrant worker context. I did not at that time realize I also had to know their Haitian context. Years later, I worked with an international development organization doing training of community workers in Port au Prince, Haiti. What a revelation! I had not seen such grinding poverty before. The sequence of my efforts in McGee's Crossroads was wrong! How could I have learned the Haitian context before designing that language teachers' course?

These men had to learn English, not only to survive in their workplace but also to consider future possibilities of continuing work in the United States, getting a green card, and ultimately becoming a citizen. Of course, I knew no Creole and it had been at least ten years since I had used French. The sequence here was clear: begin with action and move to words. This was going to be action learning: complete physical response or nothing.

A young man from MSFW who did know Creole met me at the camp and introduced me to the group of nine young Haitian men. We stood on the back porch of a wooden shack, which was to be their home while they picked tobacco and cotton for this particular North Carolina grower. We had driven through the tiny southern town of McGee's Crossroads, and folks there had glowered unhappily when they saw my car pull into the dirt road that led to the migrant camp. What was I doing there with "them"?

Today, guided by quantum thinking, which recognizes the value of a holistic approach, I would also visit with the grower and his family, getting his perspective on the problem of using Haitian workers on his land. I see how important it was for me to know the whole context, to use participation fully, including the grower and the townsfolk. Instead, I saw the grower and townsfolk as "them" even as they saw the migrant workers as "them."

Margaret Wheatley has a splendid insight that could have helped me here: "One of the principles that guides scientific inquiry is that at all levels, nature seems to resemble itself. For me, the parsimony of nature's laws gives further impetus to my desire to learn from science. If nature uses certain principles to create her infinite diversity and her well-organized systems, it is highly probable that these principles apply to human life and organizations as well. There is no reason to think that we'd be the exception. Nature's predisposition towards self-similarity gives me confidence that she can provide genuine guidance for the dilemmas of our time" (Wheatley, 1999, p. 162).

A basic principle of biochemistry is that first you prepare the ground, then you plant the selected seed. I did not honor that essential sequence but rushed into a context and social environment without adequate research and knowledge.

Barbara Kingsolver has a compelling line in *The Poisonwood Bible* (1999, p. 291): "Suppose the frigates from Arabia and Europe sailed up to the coast of Africa, looked in, and then sailed away." Suppose all of colonial or globalization efforts recognized the quantum theory that honors context and relationship, as nature does. Prepare the field before planting seed. Leave the fields fallow until they are ready. That is sequence. Quantum theory has much to offer a program planning process.

The Program and the Process

Sequence means begin at the beginning: move from small to big, slow to fast, easy to hard. We all know that. What, in this case, was small? What was slow? What was easy? I watched the pickup truck of the MSFW representative blow dust into the evening sky as he drove on to another camp, then turned shyly to the expectant group of men. I smiled. They smiled. We all leaned on the rails of the porch. There were no chairs. I laughed nervously. They laughed. Finally I said, in English, "My name is Jane. How can I say that in Creole?" Jean Pierre, who knew a little English, translated my question to the group. Everyone talked at once. Finally through the static I heard a pattern and tried to say what I had heard. "Minom ez Jeanne." They laughed even harder! Again they gave me the phrase in slow, sure Creole. Again I tried. The laughter rose. It was not laughter at me, it was sheer delight in the spectacle of this gray-haired woman making such a mash out of three little words!

I gave up on my efforts at self-identification and asked Jean Pierre (in English): "How do you say in Creole: 'Good evening? How are you?'" He told me and I tried. Side-splitting laughter, deep belly chuckles, high fives to one another accompanied by broad smiles! I tried again. And again. The laughter quieted as one by one the men tried to help me with the various sounds, repeating them for me in isolation as I struggled to get my tongue around them.

Finally, I was too tired to try any more. I wiped my sweating brow, swatted one of the million mosquitoes that were feasting on this language class, and said: "Gentlemen, You see how difficult it is for anyone to learn a new language!" Jean Pierre translated and we began with simple greetings in English, going around the porch, one by one, working in pairs to ask and respond, moving in a very slow sequence from "Hello, how are you?" "I'm fine, thanks" to a few, basic, everyday phrases. Each phrase was reinforced hundreds of times as each man repeated it.

Little did I know then that I was using an important quantum principle: energy, manifested by their spontaneity and laughter. I have always taught: no laughing, no learning. However, I did not know that was sound quantum theory. Wheatley offers this:

> Among its many influences, we can learn from new science to be more playful, to discover a new relationship with discovery. Nobel Prize winner Sir Peter Medawar says that "scientists build explanatory structures, telling stories that are scrupulously tested to see if they are stories about real life" (in Judson, 1987, p. 3). I like this idea of storytellers. It works well to describe all of us. We are great weavers of tales, listening intently around the campfire to see which stories best capture our imagination and the experience of our lives. If we can look at

ourselves truthfully in the light of this fire and stop being so serious about getting things "right"—as if there were still an objective reality out there—we can engage in life differently, more playfully. (Wheatley, 1999, p. 162)

Greetings to Home

I did not know whether they could read and write, so I asked each man to write on a clean paper the name of his wife or mother or sweetheart in Port au Prince or wherever home was in Haiti. Some wrote easily, others asked their friends to write, some wrote with great difficulty. Noting each man who could write, I immediately formed learning teams, one writer on each team.

By now they were sitting on the floor of the back porch with notebooks on their laps and stubby pencils in their hands. Here was a high-tech learning lab in McGee's Crossroads. I asked them each to find something in the house they would like to send to the person whose name they had written. They dashed into the shack and came out with transistor radios, a tin of Campbell's soup, a watch, a clock, a pillow from a bed. These were our first vocabulary words. I modeled for them a simple repetition exercise. I took one man's object: *a clock*. They repeated the word, holding and feeling the object, which they passed around the porch. "Marie." "Marie!" (Jean Pierre had written his fiancée's name, Marie.) They smiled as they read the name written on Jean Pierre's paper. "I will send." "I will send!" they repeated with alacrity. "I will send Marie a clock! He will send Marie a clock! Jean Pierre will send Marie a clock!" They laughed in joy at their sudden command of this elusive language. Each held up his object, and we went the round with *a pillow*. "Annette. I will send Annette a pillow! He will send Annette a pillow! Antoine will send Annette a pillow!" We moved happily on through Angela, Moisette, Jeanne Marie, Giselle, along with a lamp, a can of soup, a watch, a ring.

The ring got the loudest response and a great deal of teasing in Creole. Young Roberto blushed brightly under his dark skin as the group sang out: "Roberto will send Giselle a ring!" The reinforcement of the single pattern, over and over again, with variations provided by the affective response with new names and new objects, gave them control over that phrase. It was not perhaps the most useful phrase for their daily speech, but it held deep affect that would make them repeat it themselves at times. In our synthesis, at the end of the two-hour session, each man was able to say proudly: "Hello, my name is Jean Pierre. How are you? I'm fine, thanks. I will send Marie a clock!" His fellows shouted their praise as each man proved what he had learned.

Can you see how the sequence helped them learn—moving from small to big, slow to fast, easy to hard? Each time they worked together and tried those short phrases, they were reinforcing their growing knowledge and skill. Notice the other dialogue education principles at work on that back porch: respect; ideas, feelings, and actions; engagement; immediacy; relationship; and teamwork.

The next week, I arrived a bit after 7 P.M. The nine men were on the back porch, dressed as if to go to a formal event. Shoes shined, white shirts sparkling, trousers so pressed you could cut yourself on the crease. They greeted me with their chorus of English phrases. "Hello, how are you? I'm fine, thanks!" The sounds had become a bit confused, but these phrases had clearly been practiced over the week. They knew the principle of reinforcement. We continued taking small steps, using more found objects, and continuing to connect to their families in Haiti. We worked in teams, writing and reading the English words we had practiced speaking. Progress seemed excruciatingly slow to me. In their eyes, however, they were taking giant steps, adding to their repertoire of phrases and sentences that they knew they knew. I am convinced that fidelity to the principle of sequence is harder on the teacher than on the adult learner.

We spent a great deal of time on the back porch beating out the time of the phrases and sentences they were learning. "I will send Marie this clock!" Part of the sequence in language learning is hearing the idiosyncratic rhythms of the language in question. We did this by drumming on the door and walls of the back porch of their sleeping house for much of the summer. I expect they heard that rhythmic beat each time they entered that dismal shack.

A Bloody Immediate Evaluation

One evening I arrived to discover that Jean Pierre was not present. I asked about him and was told he had had two teeth extracted that day. I offered my sympathy and got on with the lesson. Suddenly, in the doorway, Jean Pierre appeared. His face was the color of old parchment, and he held a cooking pot in one hand and a wet face-cloth over his lips. He greeted me respectfully and sat down on the floor of the porch with his colleagues. He could not talk, of course, and interrupted our drumming and singsong of phrases with his coughing blood into the pot. Should I tell him he did not have to be there? Jean Pierre, however, was the subject (decision maker) of his own learning. He had made a decision. He would attend this class, and I could only celebrate his decision. He sat there through-out the class, utterly attentive, listening, smiling as well as he could in his pain, spitting blood into the cooking pan. Some indicators of success in teaching are more moving than others.

In their sense of sequence, these Haitian language students set up protocols for class night. If I arrived at 7 P.M. and they had had a long day in the tobacco fields, one would come onto the back porch and visit with me while the others showered and dressed. They never came to class in anything but their Sunday go-to-meeting clothes. If anyone were to visit our back porch language lab, they surely would have suspected that I, in my casual dress, was the migrant worker and the men were sophisticated language consultants from the Caribbean.

Evaluation of Community Response

At one point in this summer program, I decided to try to get the neighbors in McGee's Crossroads to join me in my efforts in lan-guage teaching. They could reinforce our program best by provid-ing a more human and functional site for the class than the rickety, mosquito-infested back porch. I wrote to the mayor of McGee's Crossroads, telling him of our venture and indicating that I had seen, in passing, a classroom in the back of the local fire station. How about letting us use that classroom every Tuesday night from 7 to 9? I had a quick response: "Dear Dr. Vella. We use that room every evening. Sorry."

I had to learn that the arrival of Haitian migrant workers in a small North Carolina town was part of a whole social, economic, political, and cultural history. Quantum thinking would have shown me that I was dealing with a whole not of my making. Such knowledge would have helped me understand the town's perspective of that reality.

You now are blessed with that knowledge and the resources to develop your skills in quantum thinking. In these difficult times, we can keep hope as we consider this aspect of sequence: each generation can learn from the errors of the past and can re-create history.

T. S. Eliot, in *Tradition and the Individual Talent*, (1975, p. 13), has a note about sequence that has always enchanted me. A poet can write without reference to past poetic forms. Eliot suggests that that is not poetry because there will be nothing familiar in it. A poet can repeat the past forms in his poetry. Eliot says that that is not poetry, it is repetition. A poet can take those past forms and do something creative with it. That, says T. S. Eliot, is poetry.

I recall a friend's wise advice when I, as a young woman, was heading to Tanzania to teach. I had asked her what words of wisdom she could offer me as I set off to live in a new culture, a new context. "Reserve judgment, Jane, for the first ten years!" I see now how this, too, is related to sequence. It is so easy to think that we teachers of adult learners have grasped the whole situation and, having done a learning needs and resources assessment, know all there is to know about what must be learned by this particular group. I have learned that every learning needs and resources assessment has to be open at both ends: there is always more we can learn about the situation, and we must begin somewhere. Sequence and reinforcement are useful principles that are always at work during a program.

Evaluation

Newly confident that I knew something about the situation the young teachers were getting into, I designed and led their training for the new summer program. Dr. Craige and I wrote a book for the new teachers and I dedicated it to my own best teachers: the Haitian migrant workers I had met on the back porch in McGee's Crossroads that first summer. These migrant workers followed the stream of ripening vegetables into New England, and many wove themselves into the workforce of their adopted nation as a result of their newfound language skills.

My stories of Jean Pierre and his colleagues gave the new teachers in training lots of laughs and some encouragement that they, too, could use sequence and reinforcement to enable these courageous men to learn the language and other skills that could secure their entrance into a new life. Seeing the world as I do today through the clear lens of quantum theory, I would teach those young people to go even more slowly and to learn the whole social, economic, political, and cultural environment well, for their sake and for the success of the learners.

Design Challenges

- What one thing might I have done differently to create more safety in the entire context for all the "who" involved, including the Migrant and Seasonal Farmworkers Organization, the townspeople, the grower and his family, the migrant farm workers, and the U.S. and Haitian authorities?

- What use do you see in this story of these quantum principles: the connectedness of all, energy, holistic perspectives, duality (holding the opposites), uncertainty, and participation? Knowing what you do already about quantum thinking, what one change would you make in this situation to afford the best learning for the migrant workers?

- Take any lesson you have planned: a class, a workshop, a seminar. Examine it for the occasions of reinforcement of your primary concept, skill, or attitude. How often do you repeat the idea in a new way to keep the engagement of the learner and emphasize the importance of the central point? Remember the magic number 1,142. That's how many times, I am convinced, I need to hear or do something before I know I know it.

- A principle is the beginning of an action. The principle of sequence invites us to examine our actions and reorganize them if the sequence is inappropriate. We can readily see that our sequence is not working for an adult learner when he looks confused or lost. This kind of physical indicator gives you the information you need as teacher to change your sequence with that individual or group. Stop now to reflect on a situation in which an adult learner was simply not getting something you were trying to teach. Look at the one learner. Look at your program. How could you change the distance between steps in the sequence to get that learner on board with the necessary confidence? How could you affirm and reinforce what he has already accomplished?

- The size of a group is directly related to the potential for effective reinforcement and the quality of sequence.

In this migrant labor camp I was fortunate to have a one-digit classroom: nine, not ten, adult learners. I am personally convinced that the one-digit classroom (nine, not ten learners per teacher) has tremendous potential not only for adult language learning but for the formal school system as well. Imagine the reinforcement and the personalized sequence of learning tasks that are possible in a one-digit classroom. It is an idea whose time has come.

- The principles of dialogue education are so interwoven that it is impossible not to see many at work in a situation. Two principles that are manifest in this story of the migrant labor camp in North Carolina are humor and rhythm. Again, consider any teaching you are presently doing. What was hilariously funny? How can you celebrate that? How can you bring humor into any adult learning situation? Nothing is better reinforcement than a discovery of the incongruity in a situation—the dancing light on the surface of ideas that will not fit together but dash against one another. There are endless opportunities for laughter in an adult learning situation.

- While rhythm lends itself obviously to language learning, consider how it could be used in helping adults learn whatever you are teaching. How can you use rhythm, poetry, and dance in your adult learning classes?

8

Praxis

Turning Practice into Action and Reflection

In Chapter One you read about *praxis*, a Greek word that means "action with reflection." There is little doubt among educators that adults learn by doing something with what they are learning, whether it is concepts, skills, or attitudes. Praxis is doing with built-in reflection. It is a beautiful dance of inductive and deductive forms of learning. As we know, inductive learning proceeds from the particular to the general. Deductive learning moves from the general principle to the particular situation. Both are necessary. Learning tasks can be used as praxis in teaching knowledge, skills, and attitudes as learners do something with the new knowledge, work with the new skills and attitudes, and then reflect on what they have just done. Watch how this learning event in the Maldives became praxis.

Praxis is a vital principle for effective adult learning and for dialogue learning. Engaged learners do learning tasks using new content and then do further learning tasks to reflect on what they have completed. This story of a community development training event in the island nation of Republic of Maldives shows how praxis worked for learners and teacher alike.

The Situation and the Setting

The Maldives is a small island republic stretching like a sandy Milky Way north-south in the Indian Ocean southwest of India and Sri

Lanka. There are twenty-one atolls, each with hundreds of islands that form administrative units for the government. Save the Children Federation (SCF), an international community development organization, decided to offer staff and resources for community development work in the Maldives. The government of the Maldives proposed the outlying northernmost atoll, Haa Alifu, as an impact area for the SCF staff largely because government personnel rarely got to visit any of the sixteen inhabited islands of that atoll. Michael Gibbons and Karen LeBan, codirectors of the Maldives SCF program, invited me to conduct a training program with their small staff.

Here was a development program, with many interagency links, working directly with various ministries of the government of the Maldives, ripe for field training. As usual, our lengthy correspondence prior to my arrival included my request for five days on site before the training event. These days were to be spent with Michael and Karen and whomever they named, reviewing the situation, doing a needs assessment, and designing an appropriate training program with what I learned.

We stressed the need for practical work: these community educators would make theory for themselves by reflecting on active learning. Kurt Lewin said there was nothing as practical as a good theory. I add: A good theory is handmade from action. This meant we would do the workshop in the area where Save the Children worked or someplace where program work with communities was going on. The site named by Michael and Karen was Utheem Island, one of the islands of Haa Alifu atoll, a two-day boat trip from Male, the nation's capital.

I read all I could find about the Maldives. As in so many other instances, Save the Children was seen by the government of the Maldives as a resource, bringing skills and funds to the island development program. The selection of Utheem Island as the "impact area" of Save the Children programs indicated what the government wanted: a development arm that had power and resources to reach across thousands of miles of open seas to Haa Alifu atoll. Did the government of the Maldives see this agency as an educational resource? Probably not. At that time they measured community development success in terms of buildings constructed, bridges reinforced, houses roofed. They had, however, recently opened a Center for Community Education and Development in Male. One of the participants in our training course, Mustafa Hussein, was the designated director of that new center. Perhaps this training event could link the concepts of development and education in a new way to catch the attention of the government. To this end, LeBan and Gibbons sent out an announcement to all ministries of the government, three other private voluntary organizations, and the United Nations Development Program (UNDP), inviting them to join the Save the Children training course for community development workers. Through this course they could have a new experience of doing community development through community education.

During the five days of preparation for the workshop, I had occasion to meet some of the participants from UNDP and the government. John Galace, a bright, energetic Filipino on the UNDP staff in the Maldives, was obviously going to be an important resource to the entire training project. A young field coordinator, E. E. Wijeratne from the Sri Lanka program of Save the Children, joined us from Columbo, and three young field coordinators from the Maldives Save the Children program were waiting for us in the atoll, having made the logistical preparations for our arrival. I met Mustafa Hussein, the director of the new Center for Community Development and Education, who ultimately made his learning from this training workshop available to all government programs in the islands.

Three ministries were represented: agriculture, atolls administration, and fisheries. Volunteers in Service Overseas, a British group, sent their Maldivian administrative officer. Language, as always, was a major issue. All of the group discussions during the workshop would be in Divehi, the language of the Maldives. Although tasks were set in English, they were all translated into Divehi. You will see how pictures with Divehi titles enabled us to extend the workshop throughout the whole island nation.

At the time, I saw the whole situation in Newtonian terms with emphasis on separate working parts that had to be put together. Newtonian principles led my decisions: laws control effective behavior; we value certainty and predictability; the parts completely determine the whole, so reduce the tensions in the parts and the whole will be fixed; deal with individuals and then deal with the group; hold a here-and-now focus on the actual situation; there is a subject-object split—we are subjects, the world is the object we work on; concentrate on doing, set goals, and achieve results; work on the objects in the world. You can see how such a perception of the world affected our design of training.

A quantum re-vision of that situation respects the integration of people and world. It shows that the whole is much more than the sum of the parts. As I now know, quantum thinking goes beyond the subject-object dichotomy. We recognize all people as subjects in a universe of subjects. Today the principles from quantum theory that would lead design decisions are: value uncertainty; be at ease with ambiguity; respect the individual and the group, honoring relationships as primary; celebrate that the world is also subject and in a relationship with us.

Quantum thinking helps me see that the tree outside my window, green and growing in the sun of this spring morning in North Carolina, is as beautiful as I see it to be. We do indeed evoke the world we perceive. By spending five days in preparation with the participants in the Maldives, I was actually intuitively living out these quantum principles. I just did not know what to name them at the time.

In Newtonian terms, praxis meant seeing the situation as a problem to be solved, working out the solution, and then reflecting on the outcome to draw conclusions and theory about efficient behavior. That theory would then be applied to the next problem. Quantum thinking does not see praxis so much as solving a problem as dealing creatively with a situation that has great potential as it is perceived anew by individuals and the group. The group and the individuals can flourish in relation to a situation that they create as they go. As quantum thinking tells us that we evoke the world we perceive, praxis involves not so much analysis of the indicators of a problem as heightened perception of the potential of a given situation. So the reflection part of praxis becomes not only reflection on possible causes but also more informed perception of the potential of the situation. What a different way of perceiving learning!

The Program and the Process

During the few days of preparation we had in Male before setting out on our two-day boat trip to Utheem, we used the seven steps of design to complete a specific design for the course. We studied the profile of the participants (*who*) and the situation (*why*) so that after considering the time frame (*when*) and the site near the villages (*where*), we could determine the content of the training (*what*) and set achievement based objectives (*what for*). Finally, we set tasks for the participants to do in order to learn the content (*how*). As we examined the situation, we saw that the development issues in the Maldives called for education in skills and concepts so that field staff could move from a bricks-and-mortar or construction ethic of development. We proposed a new vision of development as inviting communities to make decisions and raise resources for the improvement of their own lives.

Save the Children had been addressing this change in development direction for years, and we wanted to share our insights with other nongovernmental agencies, as well as with government and UN staff. As the new Center for Community Education was in the midst of a project to design a community development manual for the islands, Mustafa Hussein, the director, could certainly use what he would learn here. We boldly set only two simple objectives for this educational event. By the end of this workshop, participants would have (1) redefined and experienced anew the role and tasks of community development specialists and (2) designed, practiced, and evaluated community education for development. Mustafa remarked on reading these goals: "They look simple, but I expect they are not as easy as they look." Our aim was to offer participants a new experience of community development as community education. It would be a ten-day praxis that would involve direct action in the community with reflection on the theory being constructed by them.

During the ten-day workshop these men and women taught one another as they reflected together on their role in the village of Utheem. They did a community survey and began practice teaching. They came to conclusions for themselves. They knew they knew, because they had just done what they were learning. Their practice over time was becoming praxis.

On the first day, participants cited their expectations in response to this learning task: "What do you hope to learn or achieve by the end of these ten days?" They said they wanted to know

- How to encourage the community to develop through their own resources

- How to deal successfully with people

- How to share experiences for motivating poor communities

- How to make other people aware of the possibility of improving their lives

- How to satisfy leaders and laymen at the same time

- How to solve problems they face when working with the community

- How to examine and redefine their work

- How to clarify their own role

Their expectations informed the two general objectives set by us. It is the teacher's responsibility to set training objectives very clearly and explicitly for participants before the training begins. These objectives are set in the light of the learning needs and resources assessment. Then, in honest dialogue, the teacher asks adult learners what they want and need to do in light of these objectives. The dialogue begins by design.

In the middle of the ten-day session we set up an open day for rest and relaxation. This gave us, the leaders of the workshop, the chance to redesign and reshape the workshop as needed. We used that day to organize visuals for a complete synthesis of all concepts learned in the first four days. The group artist designed pictures to represent all the concepts. Since none of the course leaders wrote Divehi, a beautiful script resembling Persian, these pictorial concepts were very useful, indeed. Ultimately Mustafa Hussein produced a booklet of these pictures for use throughout the island nation.

The island site was perfect for such a training session. We were invited to use the new Mohammed Thakurufanu Memorial Center, which sat a stone's throw from the village, where participants in the training could go to do needs assessment and practice teaching. This would be excellent praxis. Each of the learning tasks we designed was a means of modeling dialogue education, which we hoped all the participants would learn and adopt. What we did in the training room is what they would do in the villages.

How could they see that the most useful image of themselves was that of teacher of the community, master of dialogue, rather than only a mason or carpenter or bridge builder? Unless they perceived their role as community development specialists anew, the villagers' dependence on them would simply grow. Our development thesis was that dependency, whether on foreign specialists or on national experts from the capital city, eats at the heart of a development process. Participants' praxis in the villages had to act in this new relationship and reflect on it (perceiving it anew) with the villagers and among themselves. This notion of praxis corroborates the quantum concept of participation: They participate as subjects in the making of this new theory of development.

Three events during the ten-day training stand out as significant aspects of participants' doing what they learned and their new perception—their praxis. The first was the community visits. In their first walk through the small community, the pairs of specialists were awkward and shy. Even Mustafa Hussein, so outgoing and talkative, was unsure what to do with the women and children he met under the shade trees around the mud and wattle houses. They reported their discomfort when they came back, and we explored new ways they could interact with the community. They tried again and again, and each time it seemed easier and more fruitful. They heard community themes more clearly. They found themselves building a relationship with the small group of womenfolk they found at home each day. This was an excellent example of praxis: the action-with-reflection cycle that is a natural way of learning. Praxis offers a special kind of community visit, full of reflection and leading to new, refined visits. It is an ongoing, never-ending cycle of change toward the potential of a given situation. These Maldivian community development specialists learned about praxis through their efforts to reach the people of the community.

The second event involved a change of plans. On the morning after their free day, which they had spent on an open boat going to a distant island, participants were not fully present to the learning tasks set out for the day. I tried to set the task and get groups started, but there was simply no energy in the group for the effort. It was 9:07 A.M. (we had started at 9 A.M.). "Let's take a short break," I suggested, much to everyone's surprise. The group dispersed, some to smoke in the courtyard, some to search for a cup of tea. They were confused by the "break" and murmured questions among themselves. I met with Le Ban and Gibbons and confessed: "I do not know what to do!" After huddling a bit, we called people back to go out, two by two, into the community to search for more themes, listen to the people, and continue their community listening survey. They came back after a few hours energized and excited by what they had heard, ready to share their research, ready to get on with the lessons in the workshop.

Here was an example of praxis. What had we learned? When you do not know what to do next, admit it and get some help from colleagues. When energy is low, get people into a physically active learning task in order to raise the energy for learning. Gibbons told me later that this was the best lesson he had ever learned about training and learning. When Mustafa Hussein asked about the sudden decision to take an early break, we explained what had happened. All of the group realized, in a unique manner, the need for physical activity when energy is low. It was a memorable lesson for us all.

The task we set for the group in order to study the concept of leadership was the third significant event of praxis. It occurred toward the end of the workshop. The small dinghy, *The Whaler*, used to move people and goods to the larger boats offshore, lay on a sandy beach on one side of the island. Its engine had been repaired and was in the boathouse near the large jetty on the other side of the island. The dinghy had to be brought around manually to the jetty in order to move the group to the large boat at high tide at 6 A.M. on the day of departure.

Here was the learning task set to the group: "In this workshop we have been considering the qualities of leadership. Now our job is to move that dinghy to the jetty." Before the task was explained any further, the group of twelve men and women rushed out the door. LeBan, Gibbons, and I followed to observe signs of leadership in the group. They reached the dinghy and pushed it into the water. Three men jumped in and began to paddle with their arms. Another fellow grabbed a long pole and began to push the boat with the pole, competing for a place in the dinghy with his friends. Another man jumped into the water to push the boat, which was by then quite full. Some of the passengers jumped out and pushed with him, and those on the beach joined in. Someone hooked an anchor into the boat, and pulled the boat using the anchor rope. The long haul around the island, through the shallow water, involved almost the entire group. A bright flag was raised (someone's shirt) and the project continued with cheers and songs. At last the group reached the distant jetty and, in a final team effort, lifted the dinghy onto the beach.

Everyone was laughing and talking excitedly as they fell, quite exhausted, onto the sand. I seized the moment to invite reflection on the learning. What did you see happen? Why do you think it happened this way? It was clear that haste was a self-imposed criterion for all the members of the group. Was this how they organized their community development work? Was the criterion: How soon can we get it done? Was that their measure of success as leaders? Clearly, there had been no design to their effort. Action people all, they set out to do the task as quickly as possible. Time had been lost and energy wasted as the strategy changed again and again. Not everyone helped, either, because people did not know their roles. It was a haphazard venture at best. This action needed reflection. This common practice needed to become praxis.

What did we learn from this? As they reflected, participants considered that the task of leaders is to organize, set out shared tasks, clarify roles, name goals, and set time limits. Leadership is not always a question of sheer sweat. It can be a question of thought. Nothing in the workshop matched this experience for richness and the potential to perceive themselves in action. A video camera capturing that scene on the beach would have greatly enriched the learning potential. We could have played that tape over and over whenever they wanted to consider the responsibilities of leadership. A voice overlay in Divehi could have made it available to any leader on the islands who had a videocassette recorder. We missed that chance.

We used this praxis to reflect on participants' ideas of a development specialist at the opening of the ten-day workshop—a person who does the job. Now they all realized the development specialist can also be a person who leads others, organizes them, inspires them, helps them determine what they want to do, and shows them how to do it most effectively.

Evaluation

Mustafa Hussein and his friends learned about themselves and achieved the first objective of the workshop: to redefine and experience anew the role and tasks of a community development specialist. As we closed the workshop, we considered the next steps. Mustafa explained that the Community Education Center was preparing a booklet on community development in Divehi, and he promised to use these concepts there. They have since produced a community education curriculum at the center using dialogue education. The curriculum of this workshop was reflected in that key educational resource.

　After a two-day journey in the launch back to Male, the group parted, assuring one another that they would continue this collaboration. Hussein led the coordination of a series of workshops for other ministries, assisted by staff from Save the Children and UNDP, during which they taught what they had learned on Utheem. The community development booklets produced in Divehi for the entire country reflected a dialogue approach to adult learning and development. All the concepts and skills learned on Haa Alifu atoll were included through a series of charming illustrations, making them accessible to both literate and preliterate island workers. Hussein had been right: the two objectives of the community development workshop in the Maldives had indeed been achieved. And they were not at all as simple as they looked.

This experience with a small group of community education people proved again that the most complex concepts can be learned best by active involvement with the learning process. When the "leaders" felt embarrassed about their chaotic efforts to move the boat and took time to perceive how they could have used the potential of that situation, they were learning. They were making theory they could use. When we finished the action and the reflection of that learning task, they knew that they knew. I could say with assurance that they had demonstrated a new way of looking at community development as education. When Mustafa Hussein and his friends took the concepts, skills, and attitudes of the workshop, turned them into a participative workshop in Divehi, produced a picture book for development workers in the islands, and taught others, they knew that they knew those concepts, skills, and attitudes. When the group discovered how intimidating their presence in the village was—and then organized to adapt their ways of greeting the women and talking with them—they learned how to do a community survey. Praxis offered them the experience and the opportunity to reflect on their experience together. They learned that their relationship with one another and with the villagers was the basis of their work. Mustafa Hussein put it clearly: "We see now that change is from the heart!"

Design Challenges

- *Praxis* is the Greek word for "action with reflection." How would you now define or describe praxis for your colleagues? In your teaching and in the design of your programs, how can you use the concept and practice of praxis to energize adult learners and invite them to significant learning? Remember that a learning task is praxis when it includes not only significant action but also time for reflection on that action.

- Examine the following critical incident. Decide how this frustrated teacher could use praxis to bring the group to more effective learning of skills and knowledge of new computer programs.

Howard is a computer instructor at a community college. He has a large class of thirty young men and women who are being taught to use the Internet. For the first three sessions, Howard lectures the group on the development of the Internet, its history, and new applications. At the fourth lesson, only half of the group attends. Howard is angry and tells those present how grateful they should be for this opportunity to learn a vital resource.

Use these open questions to learn from Howard's dilemma:

1. What do you see happening here?
2. Why do you think it is happening?
3. When this happens when you are teaching, what will be the results for the adult learners?
4. What have you learned about praxis and dialogue education from the example in the Maldives that you might share with Howard so that he might reach all the students?

9

Learners as Decision Makers
Harnessing the Power of Self Through Respect

In Chapter One you read about the power that is unleashed in
adult learners when they feel they are respected as subjects or decision makers of the learning event. Respecting learners as subjects
or decision makers of their own learning is a principle that involves
the recognition that adults are, in fact, decision makers in a large
part of their lives. Healthy adults desire to be respected as subjects
and resist being treated as objects, something that can be used by
another. In dialogue education we assume that people are not designed to be used by others. Adults as subjects of their own learning need to know that, insofar as possible, they themselves decide
what occurs for them in a learning event.

In this story of Durga of Nepal, we examine this principle of respect at work. Nepal is a magnificently beautiful country of vast
mountain ranges and rolling lowlands, with strong-legged and
strong-minded people who have maintained their unique culture
for millennia. The young man who is the hero of this story, Durga
Bahadur Shrestha, is a striking example of the integrity and intelligence of Nepali youth.

The Situation and the Setting

The question I asked myself as we began the training-of-trainers
workshop for Save the Children field staff in Nepal was a tough one.

How can an American woman teacher invite a group of young Nepali men and women, the field staff of a community development organization, to become more effective adult educators in a period of two weeks? One thing was sure: the design would have to respect the learners as decision makers, subjects of their own learning and development. They would decide what principles and practices would work for them.

It was the German philosopher Hegel who spoke against perceiving human beings as objects and not as they truly are, subjects—decision makers—in their own lives. He was writing in the midst of the Industrial Revolution, when men were considered "hands" on the assembly line. The idea of being subject of one's own life is a powerful one. I have observed learners from many cultures resonate with the potential as they reflected on their experience of being decision makers in their own learning and their own lives. Perhaps this is so because in many cultures men and women have, indeed, been treated as objects. We are designed as human beings to be subjects.

The content of a course is sheer potential, waiting for learners and teacher to develop it to fit their context. At the completion of the second training-of-trainers course that I led with the field staff of Save the Children in Nepal, I asked the group how they thought they had changed during the weeks of training. Durga smiled his delightful smile and pointed proudly at himself, saying, "Subject!"

The program and projects of Save the Children in Nepal lie in an area many miles north of the field office in Katmandu. Durga's task is to coordinate health education programs in Takukot, some fourteen hours from the capital. This agency often works in the more remote areas, where government services are rare and the need is greatest. This means that the field staff—nurses, agriculturists, community development specialists, water engineers, housing specialists, road builders—all must be self-directed and self-monitored team workers who are indeed decision makers in their own lives. How could a training program for professional field staff emphasize their responsibility to invite villagers to be such decision makers (subjects) of the community development programs in these Himalayan mountains of Nepal? What could we do to invite that smile and that expression of self-confidence, "Subject!" from all?

Community development in Nepal is a complex affair owing to the rough terrain of the country. The glorious Himalayas are home to thousands of small communities of mountain farmers who make their living in agriculture, fishing, and livestock. This is a unique setting for learning. When we speak of the setting, we mean all those aspects of the environment that make or break the educational opportunity for learners. Distances in Nepal are major obstacles. To get a sick child to a hospital may mean a two- or three-day trek down dangerous mountain slopes. To market a crop of tomatoes, the farmer walks a vertical track to urban centers such as Katmandu or Gorka. Imagine a toothache six days' walk away from a dentist!

The community development programs in the area had matured over eight years. The staff worked with sensitivity and empathy to form a viable, durable program in the distant mountain outposts of Dhuwakot, Deurali, Pandrung, and Mahjlakuribot. The Katmandu field office directed and serviced these mountain programs. I had been invited by Gary Shea, the American Field Office director, to design and conduct a staff development program with Nepali field staff. I was new at the time to Save the Children and had a great deal to learn about the settings of such training events. I did ask that the training take place in a field site so that there would be ample opportunity to do teaching practice in the villages.

On the second day of our trek into the Himalayas, we arrived at the training site: a remote and desolate mountainside a few miles north of the village of Pandrung where Save the Children had a small office. Thirty field staff from all the mountain programs met us there. Some of them anticipated the staff development program with curiosity and excitement. Some were frankly alarmed at the prospect of living for two weeks in tents on the mountainside. Durga offered a warm welcome to all of us to his impact area, which had overnight become the agency's mountainside training center.

The Sherpa staff set to work with experienced efficiency and prepared a tent camp: dining tent, sleeping tents spread along the sides of the mountain, kitchen tent, latrines built into the hillside. As educator I wondered: Where in the world are we going to teach? The villages around were wonderful for practical work, but where would we gather for the sessions? We could have used the one large tent that served as a dining room. I decided that we should not. We had to respect the learners' need for relaxation and distance from the work at least at mealtimes. They needed this large tent for rest and relaxation as a gathering place, a "living room."

On the way to the campsite we had passed a rather charming, if dilapidated, cowshed that looked like a scene from an old Christmas card. The roof of mud and wattle slanted to the ground; the floor was covered with dirty straw; there were no walls. One could sit on the floor of the shed and see miles and miles of Himalayan mountains all the way toward Tibet and China. There were no animals in this stable. A footpath passed by the shed, used by villagers on their way to and from the little town four miles away. When I inquired, Durga explained that the stable belonged to an old farmer whose cows had all been sold.

I had immediately thought of this old cowshed as a possible training site, but I knew this decision could not be mine. I was not the decision maker because I did not know enough about Nepali customs. The group had to decide. The learners had to be the subjects of this staff development program even at this point. Their voice on this matter was deliberative (decisions), not merely consultative (suggestions). I invited Durga and his colleagues to search for an appropriate site for our sessions in the vicinity of our camp. They left in small groups, somewhat confused by the assignment, somewhat bemused by this strange American woman in their midst. They came back to report that they had discovered an old cowshed they wanted me to look at with them. They were apprehensive, however, that my own cultural taboos would not allow us to use an abandoned mud-and-wattle stable. Perhaps they did not make the Christmas card connection. When we looked at it together, we decided it was not only convenient to the camp but also large enough and bright enough for our work. We all agreed to clean it up at once. They named it *gaiko got:* "the place of learning." A carpet of clean straw, an easel tucked into the corner under the low roof with a large chart full of Nepali characters, a scattering of mats from the tents, and our place of learning was ready. Their having made this decision, and my having corroborated it, got the training-of-trainers workshop off to a very good start. Participants experienced what it felt like to be decision makers of at least one important variable: the setting of the training. Later, when we spoke of the principle of seeing villagers as subjects, they could use this experience to test the authenticity of the concept. This was Durga's first public experience as leader of all the field staff. He discovered how it felt to make a sound decision with the group.

This experience was also exquisite praxis. We began with the experience of searching together, examined our decision as we perceived the potential on that mountainside, then changed our knowledge set to incorporate the new learning. As we learned in Chapter Eight, praxis is action with reflection. Praxis is the basis of learning among subjects via the dialogue approach. How significant it was that the first action of the Nepal field staff participating in the workshop was to decide where we were to work for the next two weeks. I realized anew how important it is to use such real-life situations to teach and learn.

The setting of this unique training of trainers in Nepal was a key variable in the workshop's success. As we saw in Chapter Three, when we use the seven steps of design, we are asked to respect the significance of the learning site *(where)*. Our arrangement of the site or context is a way of respecting the learners as subjects of their own learning.

The Learners

An experienced group of community development fieldworkers and managers gathered that first morning in our cowshed classroom. Virtually all of the field staff had university degrees in their respective disciplines: agriculture, nutrition, health, nursing, engineering, community development, or management. All had studied in a formal setting in high school and university. Their idea of education came from that formal setting. This workshop would give them an alternative approach more appropriate for the village settings in which they worked.

The participants came to these communities as the experts from Katmandu. It was entirely understandable for them to offer solutions to the villagers, give answers even before the questions could be asked, and thus unwittingly treat the villagers as objects of their own professional decisions. These field staff were more than experts in their disciplines, however. They were also sensitive human beings, grassroots educators whose experience in the field helped them realize that their solutions often did not work. They had all lived through classic development problems: water systems they built went untended, agricultural advice went unheeded, children continued to die as mothers failed to change their traditional maternal practices.

These field staff recognized that their formal educational practices were not always effective. They had come miles and miles to this hillside, this learning place, to discover together the dialogue approach to community education for villagers. Although they did not entirely understand what this new approach entailed, they had been willing to trek to this place from their outposts in order to spend two weeks learning new knowledge, skills, and attitudes. Most of the participants knew some English. We decided that whatever dialogue we had would be in Nepali. We had three or four members who could translate from English into Nepali and back. It would slow down the process considerably, but that in itself was a good thing. We Americans were known in Nepal as "the quick ones," apparently famous for wanting to achieve more than is possible or desirable in a given time. We needed to have the learners themselves set the pace of training. Why? Education and training are only as good as they are accountable. If at the end of the two weeks I had "covered" a set of theories and skills but the participants could not demonstrate their grasp of those theories and skills, the program would not have been accountable. Considering where we were, on the slopes of the Himalayas miles from Katmandu, this program had to be 100 percent accountable. Such a staff development opportunity would not soon come again.

It was imperative for me to model, in all aspects of the program, the use of the principles, skills, and behaviors being taught. We had to do what we were teaching. This is a great advantage of such adult education settings. There is neither time nor place for empty words. Paulo Freire of Brazil calls such empty words, "a hollow, alienated, and alienating verbosity" (Freire, 1972, p. 57). Freire points out that such verbalism is the result of theory without adequate action. Since translation is precarious at best, we had to make sure that each command for each task being translated could be proven in actions. If the learners did what was being asked, we would know the translation was accurate. Such an arrangement helped me be very clear and simple in setting learning tasks. Again, the learners were subjects of this event: they themselves naturally decided what they heard and what they had to do. I, too, was a subject, deciding how to set the learning tasks. However, I was not the only subject, nor the only teacher, in the cowshed.

The ages, educational background, and experience of the group were varied. This diversity raised another question: How do we decide which skills, knowledge, and attitudes are appropriate for the entire group? To whom do we aim the training—to the more experienced or to the younger set? In Chapter Four, where we studied training in Ethiopia during the famine, we examined the concept and skill of learning needs and resources assessment. Here in Nepal, the breadth of the learning needs and resources of this group made the decision a tough one. I finally decided to present a very basic course aimed at the younger set, inviting the more accomplished to serve as senior partners in the learning.

Villagers proved to be part of the learning community, as well, not only during the practical work but also as they trudged along the path that circled the cowshed. One day late in the second week as we were reflecting together on a design that had been tried the previous evening in the nearby village, an old woman passed by with a great pile of wood strapped to her bent back. She mumbled something as she passed that made the young men chuckle. "What did she say?" I asked. They were still laughing as they translated her disgruntled murmuring: "Talk, talk, talk," she had said. "All they do is talk, and we . . . we learn nothing!"

We stopped the learning task to reflect humbly on her feedback of our process. How were we "speaking" to the communities on the hillside who observed our work in the cowshed day after day? What were we communicating to them? The water engineer proposed that we take a day from our course to repair the water system that served these villagers. We all enthusiastically agreed. Teacher and staff spent the next day knee-deep in mud and rocks repairing the walls, securing the platform, resetting the pipes in the mountain so that the water flowed smoothly without interruption. Exhausted, hot, dirty, and deeply gladdened by our sense of accomplishment, the group gathered for supper at the camp after completing the job. Some of the participants were concerned that we had lost one day of the workshop. I had to respond: "My friends, we did not lose a day from our course. For me, this was one of the most useful learning tasks in the whole workshop! What did today mean to you?"

We heard a fascinating set of responses to that question emphasizing the need to present immediate results to the village communities where the participants work. One man said, "I learned anew how hard it is to work together." Another, a woman who does health programs, declared that she and her staff were going to do something equally visible and tangible when she returned to her field post. As subjects of their own lives and work, they were applying the day's lesson to their future. They had made theory that they could now practice.

The Program and the Process

Before my arrival in Nepal, the fieldworkers who were to do the training-of-trainers course completed a short survey form:

1. What do you hope to have learned at the end of this two-week course?

2. What do you hope to have practiced?

3. What do you see as the most critical problem facing villagers in your area?

As we collated these responses, I learned participants' perspectives on the needs of villagers. The issue of women's "ignorance" was mentioned by six participants. Five mentioned villagers' lack of awareness and general poverty. Four mentioned lack of trained personnel in the villages and lack of community organization. Three spoke of the need for clean drinking water, developing local leadership, and learning how to maintain development programs. Many mentioned illiteracy. They wanted to learn how to motivate villagers, how to do program design, how to get participation in a meeting. They wanted to learn training and evaluation methods. They wanted to learn the goals and history of the agency (Save the Children USA) and discover why it was in Nepal. They asked how to design and conduct effective meetings and how to maintain programs once they were in place. They wanted to master communication skills, learn how to do a community analysis, and develop leadership skills and self-reliance in the community.

This was a formidable and sophisticated set of learning needs for a two-week workshop. Indeed, it could have been a curriculum for a master's degree course in rural development. The group indicated how keen they were to learn. In light of their responses to the survey, I was able to structure a workshop that reflected their basic needs. Again, they were subjects, along with me, in naming the content and objectives of this training event. This was an essential aspect of the modeling I promised to do. I demonstrated that it is possible to have a set of basic content and objectives for a training, enter into a dialogue with the learners about their context, and then adapt the course to the context. When people see that you are listening and that they are indeed decision makers with you, their motivation changes dramatically.

On the first day during our initial meeting in the cowshed, we reviewed in Nepali a final set of achievement based objectives. By the end of this two-week session, all participants would have

- Reviewed current adult learning theory

- Prepared a community map of this area and participants' own impact area

- Conducted a learning needs and resources assessment with villagers in this area

- Distinguished between monologue and dialogue

- Examined relationships for development and learning

- Practiced using open questions

- Designed educational events for the villages, using dialogue and the seven steps of design (these would be discipline-specific)

- Designed appropriate learning materials

- Prepared achievement based objectives for each event

- Used all the principles of dialogue learning in their teaching

- Distinguished learning, transfer, and impact

- Named immediate and long-term indicators for learning, transfer, and impact

- Discovered or designed further learning resources

After participants reviewed these achievement based objectives, we asked a further set of questions:

1. What is missing among these objectives?

2. What is not necessary or irrelevant from your perspective?

3. Which three objectives are most important to you in your job?

Such open questions enabled the small groups to speak honestly, cite their priorities, and listen as others named theirs. Asking an open question assumes a variety of perspectives within the group and invites learners to speak as subjects of their own learning. By the end of the morning, we had a set of objectives named by the group as priorities, named by me as basic, and agreed to by all. These were our workshop objectives. We had set our own agenda as subjects of our own learning. It was quite an achievement, well worth the hours involved. We all knew from experience that these objectives would change and grow during the two weeks (witness the repair of the village water system!). Paradoxically, such changes and such growth can only take place when achievement based objectives and content are explicit, specific, and clear. These are quantum concepts at work: duality and uncertainty.

We learned a great deal about individual perspective in this learning task. I took the opportunity to explain how perspective was translated in Swahili as *msimamo*, "the place where one stands." Nouns in Swahili belong to classes or categories. This word should have been a place word, *pasimamo*, but in fact it is an m-word, *msimamo*. The m-class words in Swahili are words like person *(mtu)*, mountain *(mlima)*, river *(mto)*, tree *(mti)*. These are all places where the spirit lives. We can conclude that Africans understood that a person's perspective is a holy place to be honored and respected, even if it is different from another's. Since we are designed to be subjects of our own lives and to treat the world as a subject growing by our dialogue, our personal perspective is vital for us to understand, accept, and honor. This is quantum thinking. We do indeed evoke the world we perceive.

We had demonstrated the difference between "banking" (monologue) and "problem-posing" (dialogue) approaches to community education—as described by Paulo Freire in his *Pedagogy of the Oppressed* (1972)—and they recognized the dialogue we had been modeling in this event all along. Freire speaks of "codification of limit situations," showing how a teacher using these dialogue approaches can present the real-life situation to a group through a code—a picture, story, or sociodrama—and then use open questions to "decodify" the situation and offer facts and skills to deal with it (Freire, 1972, p. 103). I have always found such language difficult. There had to be a simpler way to put it. The Nepali staff spontaneously gave us that simpler way: they called the principles and practices they were learning "tools for development." I was delighted to see the Nepali staff, as subjects of their own learning, take over the language of the learning experience, not only by translating the concept into Nepali but also by simplifying the academic jargon into words that worked for them. They not only made theory; they also formed that theory in accessible language.

A Warm-Up for Subjects

We started the program early the first morning in the cowshed by inviting participants to do a warm-up: form teams of twos with someone from another post and select a single thing that symbolized their work in Nepal. They had five minutes to find that thing and decide how they would present their symbol to the others.

People presented a shovel, stones, pieces of water pipe, a live chicken, a book, an egg. Each item was seen to represent their work as community education officers. The motley collection symbolized what the agency was trying to do with rural villagers in the mountains of Nepal. Each team was acting as decision makers. No one rejected any symbol. No symbol was better than any other. The design of the task invited equal sharing. There was the inevitable constructive and productive competition as the teams worked to select a meaningful symbol. This competition simply added energy and motivation to the task. Each team finished in five minutes. Teams presented their symbols briefly and with good humor. No one was left out as each team introduced itself through its symbols. Every symbol was lavishly affirmed and applauded.

Although this can be seen as a simple warm-up activity, it had great weight in the program. It got people working together who did not know one another well. Participants had come from different outposts scattered throughout the mountains. They were experts in different disciplines: agriculture, health, water, and women's programs. The activity got them to make decisions and use their creative imagination under time pressure. The experience taught them what happened when their ideas were welcome and affirmed. This *gaiko got* was seen to be a safe learning place.

Durga and his companion selected a hoe as their symbol, showing how the agricultural programs not only provided nutrition to families and funds from market produce but also were organizing tools to get farmers to study and work together. The agriculturists organized meetings of men and women farmers to teach new techniques and distribute improved seeds and fertilizers. As neither Durga nor his colleague were agriculturists, their symbol encouraged the agricultural specialists among the field staff, since it came from their peers and colleagues from other disciplines. A major fact in motivation is that advice or praise from a peer carries more weight than advice, correction, or praise from an outsider or a manager. There is a certain validity in the estimation of colleagues who know how hard you have worked to organize a course or do field visits, because they have done it themselves. The affirmation they heard in the cowshed became a function of the new culture of this organization.

In modeling this dialogue approach, we used a largely inductive design. To teach communication skills, for example, we first used a simple game, "pass the message," without offering a theoretical system for feedback or checking. We set time limits so the message, "Meet me at the Bissani Hotel in Gorhka on Thursday, April 25, at 2 P.M. to trek to Pandrung," would surely be garbled before it reached the end of the line. The message that was finally received after a speedy, unsystematic passage from person to person was,

"Meet your brother at Katmandu." Everyone had a good laugh at their own expense and recognized that such miscommunication often happens in their work and lives.

We then used the four open questions:

1. What do you see happening here?
2. Why do you think it is happening?
3. When it happens in your life, what follows?
4. What do you think we can do about it?

These questions move from perception to reflection on causes to application to one's own life to resolution. They demand that all learners act as subjects, deciding what the situation means to them and what might resolve it. This is also praxis. After deciding that a system of checking was needed as the message was passed and that writing such a message was the best method of checking, the group tried to pass a second message. It arrived safely, whole and intact. They were quite surprised. This activity offered empirical evidence of the usefulness of checking communications. It was an experience of inductive learning—of praxis.

Groups of three were then invited to design a similar learning game for the use of village leaders. Many of the groups used music and song in their "development tools." Once the creative imagination was stimulated in a safe setting where there was no judging and where working in a team made personal responsibility less burdensome, learners proved themselves creative and productive. This has been my experience all around the world: control the variables and people will produce. They will be content to work hard on their own tasks. What are those variables? They are essentially the principles and practices of dialogue education, twelve of which are offered in this book. See Vella (1995) for a set of fifty principles. These principles and practices are so hinged that you cannot use one without invoking another. Some of the principles that were working in the *gaiko got* were safety, clarity of task, appropriate timing, respect for the learners and content, praxis, engagement, and lavish affirmation.

It was hot and dusty in our cowshed. The rain made a mountain of mud on occasion. The working days were long. People were away from their homes and families. These variables could not be controlled. Despite all this, however, learners were motivated—by the safety, the clear tasks, the relevance of knowledge and skills being learned, the respect offered both them and the results of their learning tasks—to produce their own learning with alacrity and generosity.

A History Lesson for Subjects

The Nepali field staff wanted to know why this organization (Save the Children) was in Nepal and what they as staff represented to their village clients and neighbors. How can you use dialogue education to teach the history and goals of an agency? Our "development tool" was a story that they had to complete in teams of three: a description of the beginnings of the agency through the invitation received by SCF from the king and queen of Nepal in 1980. Teams had to resolve this question: Why choose Gorkha district for a work area? How would you select a community for Save the Children to work in? They had in the story a set of criteria for selection of work areas and a list of possible villages. But all the facts were presented as an open system for their consideration. The opinion of these field staff members on the shape of the program in Nepal was invited and respected. Heatedly they debated some of those opinions, and in the debate they clarified their own understanding. They were engaged in learning and also in constantly creating the agency's role in Nepal. This was such good quantum thinking! By their fieldwork they were in fact constantly restructuring their specific role in their villages. This is the meaning of the quantum concept of participation: *as subjects we evoke the world.* It was our hope that this theoretical dialogue would inform their fieldwork as their experience informed the theory. It was an exciting dialogue among subjects.

In all the activities of the workshop, the principle of participants' being respected as subjects was operative. They decided
which villages they would work in for practice teaching, what to
teach, how to design a "development tool" appropriate for the
group, and how to invite feedback from the group on their learning. Since this group of staff represented only a quarter of the entire field staff of the Nepal field office, it was also necessary for them
to prepare to teach their colleagues in Katmandu what they were
learning. Again, by modeling a dialogue approach throughout, I
gave them a basis for the training-of-trainers workshops they would
conduct when they returned to their own work areas.

Evaluation: Transfer Is Immediate

On a Sunday afternoon toward the end of the training, pairs were
sent out to visit families in nearby villages in order to listen further
for the issues of the villagers—their themes. This is what Durga and
his companion reported: "We found a family in a house with a bro-
ken smokestack. The owner was angry because the smokestack was
not working. We found an old father sick on a bed upstairs. When
we visited him we saw that he was taking local medicine. Durga told
a story of a friend of his who was very sick and took local medicine
and got much worse. When we talked more with the old man, he
said he planned to have his son take him to the health clinic to get
new medicine."

I was delighted to see how Durga had internalized elements of
dialogue education: not scolding the sick old man but using a story
to beguile him with possibilities. How quickly Durga had composed
that "development tool," the story of his imaginary friend, at the
old man's bedside! It demonstrated Durga's ability with this approach. This was immediate transfer—a sound indicator for evaluation of Durga's learning.

During the feedback session at the end of the program, the staff
indicated that the distinction between monologue and dialogue was

one of the most useful things they had learned in the workshop. A lovely closure, using music and song, was designed by Rham Bal, a gifted young engineer. The lyrics included a chorus in Nepali, "We sing honor to . . ." and each person in the workshop was named with appropriate lyrics about his or her contribution to the workshop.

Longitudinal Evaluation: Impact

After this training of trainers, participants gave a number of short training sessions to their colleagues so that dialogue education became the pattern of this agency field program. Among senior staff there was general agreement that this approach and this philosophy of community development were appropriate for the Nepal situation.

Two years later, one of the participants, K. G. Deepak, a field coordinator, prepared a significant study demonstrating how field staff were working with communities toward turning responsibility for community development over to leaders and members of the local village group. This turnover of control to national and local leadership was recognized as a result of the use of dialogue among the staff and in the communities. Only people who have practice in acting as subjects of their own lives can take responsibility for programs and resources so as to hand over control to others. Two years after the training workshop, I had the joy of returning to Nepal to do a "training for turnover" that reinforced basic community development skills. This occasion presented an opportunity for a group of field staff to design a comprehensive training of trainers with me for the growing number of new staff. It was at this time that Durga indicated he was confident of his being "subject."

Reflections: Subjects in a Participatory World

What strikes me now is the development of my own skills, concepts, and behaviors through this work. What I know now about doing such a training of trainers is substantially more than what I knew at the first Nepal workshop. Who taught me this added knowledge? I see that my teachers were Durga and his colleagues from the mountains of Nepal, who were in turn taught by the villagers. Perhaps the best part of this dialogue approach is that the teacher learns, changes, and grows.

Zohar points out: "A quantum entity must always be seen within the larger context of its defining relationships. Change the context and the entity itself is different" (1997, p. 46). When we create a safe, challenging learning context where men and women know they are seen as subjects of their own learning, they become what they are and what they always knew they could be.

Design Challenges

- Consider your own experience of learning in high school, college, a professional training program, or graduate school. At what moment did you feel entirely a subject of your own learning? When did you make the decisions about what you were to learn and how you were to learn it? If you did not feel like a decision maker in a program, consider what the instructor might have done to invite you to be subject of that learning. How does this relate to what you are now doing in your teaching programs? How can you use the quantum principle of participation to design your programs?

- What are the political implications of such a design for dialogue? How will you deal with the new learning-teaching relationships that will evolve if you use these principles? These principles seem so simple that it is very easy to say: *I know all this! I have been doing this for years.* But we have discovered that those who say they know have the least ability to learn. How can we stay open to the potential for growth and creativity, to the kind of transformative change that might occur as we implement the principles and practices of dialogue learning?

- In your own work, how do you honor the learners as subjects of their own learning?

- What would show you that a group of learners is feeling more confident about themselves as subjects? How can you celebrate such new ways of acting toward the content, toward you as teacher, and toward one another?

10

Learning with Ideas, Feelings, and Actions

Using the Whole Person

You read in Chapter One a description of the principle that guides us to be aware of the cognitive-affective-psychomotor aspects in the design of effective adult learning. By using the principle that there are three aspects of learning—ideas (cognitive), feelings (affective), and actions (psychomotor)—we can ensure engagement of learners. We know that most learning involves more than cognitive material (ideas and concepts). It involves feeling something about the concepts (emotions) and doing something (actions). Whether I am learning the concept of stakeholders in strategic planning, or the skill of playing the piano, or the attitude of confidence when addressing an audience, I need to consider all three aspects: cognitive, affective, psychomotor—ideas, feelings, actions.

Bloom's classic taxonomy of educational objectives (1956) offers a clear distinction among cognitive, affective, and psychomotor objectives. He distinguishes objectives for teaching ideas, attitudes, and skills. The principle we examine in this chapter is the usefulness of making every learning task engage learners on all three levels at once. These elements need not be distinct; they can be, and often are, integrated. When you are teaching a concept, consider how the learning task can also elicit the learners' feelings about the concept. How can the learning task invite them to do something with the concept? The more we integrate all three elements, the more critical the learners will be about the significance of the learning in their context and the better the concept can be integrated into their lives.

The wholeness of all nature and the connectedness of all things demonstrated by quantum theory is what I now recognize as the basis of this principle. These aspects of learning are as interconnected as body and soul, as earth, air, fire, and water. When we want to help people learn, we must use all three aspects: ideas, feelings, and actions. Kurt Lewin taught this: Effective learning will affect the learner's cognitive structures, attitudes and values, and perceptions and behavioral patterns. That is, it always involves cognitive, affective, and psychomotor factors (in Johnson and Johnson, 1991, p. 54).

Such integration can avoid the fragmentation that can impede learning. I return here to the concept of praxis as experience with reflection toward enhanced perception of the meaning of that experience. The learner, through an integrated learning task, can grasp the meaning of the concept or the skill being learned. Fritjof Capra explains his need to invite quantum thinking by recognizing "that our crisis is a crisis of *perception*" (1983, p. 2). Lewin suggests that personal learning cannot be effected without dealing in all three aspects: ideas, skills, and attitudes. Donald Oliver adds to the dialogue with his distinction between technical and ontological knowing. He maintains that our society is brilliant in technical knowing but not as effective in ontological knowing (Oliver, 1989 p. 14). The principle we are studying here is the forceful one that holds that an effective learning task of either technical or ontological learning involves concepts, skills, and attitudes, that is, ideas, actions, and feelings. It has cognitive, psychomotor, and affective elements.

The Story and the Setting

The integration of ideas, feelings, and actions is the focus of this story of young Mikaeli Okolo, his Zambian colleagues, and his missionary mentors from Europe. Okolo is a young Zambian who was educated in theology in Lusaka, Zambia, and then did graduate work in sociology in Rome. He uses his doctorate as parish priest in a small mountain village in northern Zambia. I met him at a leadership training workshop offered by the Zambian Episcopal Conference to a selected group of Zambian and foreign clergy. I had been invited to design and lead the workshop.

It was with some apprehension that I accepted that invitation from Dick Cremins, a Jesuit priest from the Zambian Episcopal Conference. He wanted me to work with this group of church leaders on methods of dialogue education. He called it "leadership training" and entitled the workshop: "Equality: The People of God as the Church of God." These men and women had all read Paulo Freire's *Pedagogy of the Oppressed* and wanted to know how to use these challenging ideas in their pastoral work. The very idea of missionary teaching seemed to stand in stark contradiction to the dialogue approach, the education of decision-making subjects, suggested by Freire. I took heart from my own apprehension and doubts, however, recognizing that I could not do much "teaching" about an educational approach from this wise personal base of tentative searching. Whenever I start a class or a course, in my own country or in another setting stranger to me, I recall with a smile the story of a medieval saint. On arriving at the town walls of a new site for his ministry, he got off his dusty old horse and knelt to pray: "Let me do as little harm as possible to the people in this town."

The group had been called from among pastoral leaders throughout Zambia. They had already had some training in the Freire-based process of community education and all had a constituency of Zambian Christians with whom they worked. They had already designed some leadership training programs themselves and were using them with these parishioners. They trusted Dick Cremins, so they came to work with me on his recommendation. There was, unfortunately, little learning needs assessment done in preparation for this workshop except for a series of sporadic conversations between me and Cremins. This one man was much too small a sample, however, and as a church bureaucrat his perspective was not that of the parish priests. The time frame for preparation was such that I knew I would have to find out about the group during the first days of the six-day session.

The Learners

The group I met at the Zambian retreat house outside Lusaka was as Irish as it was Zambian! A majority of Irish Jesuit priests and brothers, along with a sprinkling of other European clergy, represented the missionary leadership of the Zambian church. A small number of Zambian priests, brothers, and nuns rounded out the group.

We began as usual by telling our personal stories to one another in small groups and then sharing significant aspects of these stories in the larger group. At the same time we shared our hopes and fears for this week. Everyone spoke of the hope of learning specific ways to work effectively with their "people," their "parishioners." They wanted practical models for daily work—this much was clear. An undercurrent of feeling was just as clear: on the one hand, they all wanted more clarity of their role; on the other hand, they were all afraid someone would tell them what that role was. Many of the Irish priests had been professors of the young Zambians when they had been in seminary. These Irishmen had been reared in the absolute hierarchical culture of a religious order. They had taught young Zambians, who were now working quite independently in rural, distant, isolated "bush" parishes.

How can one examine the potential of human beings to see themselves as subjects, decision makers in their own lives, when both culture and a harsh morality put the decision making in another's hands? This was not an abstract issue. On the very first day, evidence arose to demonstrate that this pain was being felt then and there. If, as we learn in quantum physics, context is operative, the context of that international, culturally complex Zambian situation was working on all involved.

The Program and the Process

Dialogue, learning tasks, and reading went along on the first and second days as designed. I began to see, however, significant gestures that told me we were not yet addressing what they needed to learn. At one point, small groups had prepared some creative material as a model for parish work. As one group began its report, the young Zambian, Okolo, got up to describe the group's work. An Irish Jesuit in the same group said to his Irish colleague, "Tom, why don't you give the report? It will be easier for everyone to understand." Tom took the paper from the hands of the startled Zambian, who sat down in shock and shame. No one in the room commented on the incident, nor did anyone oppose what had occurred. Ironically, the subject of the report was equality.

I had to make a quick judgment call. Should I act on this or not? Not yet, I cautioned myself. This is too deep. Get more evidence. I was right. The evidence flowed freely. At tea, there was a remarkable self-imposed color bar. Irish chatted with Irish, Zambians with Zambians. At meals, tables were mixed but conversation was not. The men talked to the men; women were often excluded. The Zambians talked to one another, Irish talked to Irish, Dutch to Dutch. The latter even used their own language at times in a mixed group. As presentations were made during the course, the same phenomenon appeared. A woman rarely represented a small group. If we had made a video of the program, the evidence would have been irrefutable. I could not possibly record here all the instances of blatant but unconscious ethnocentrism and sexism.

The theme of the workshop, as noted, was "Equality: The People of God as the Church of God." Abstractions flowed from the lips of these old priests like honey. They were utterly unconscious of the contradiction they were living both in their work and at this workshop.

Starpower: A Simulation About Inequality

I knew we had to get out of our heads. We had to bring in the affective and psychomotor elements. But how could we do this appropriately? That was my challenge. The principle I used was the one we are studying, taught by Kurt Lewin: meshing the cognitive issue with learners' affective response and psychomotor activity. I had to respect their roles and their culture, of course, and the hierarchy that was present. I had to trust that they, too, could be subjects of their own coming to consciousness, of their enhanced perception.

They had all been deeply moved by the political and economic colonialism that Africa had suffered for hundreds of years. The learning simulation Starpower (1993) offers a threefold consideration of colonialism: ideas, feelings, and actions are called into play as groups are formed in the simulation and then put into an adversarial win-lose challenge. I introduced the simulation as one I had frequently used with great success in having people come to understand the effects of class antagonism. I offered it to them with the caveat that they should test it as learning material and decide in task groups how it could be adapted for use in Zambian rural parishes.

They entered the simulation wholeheartedly. And each discovered, in accord with the design of the simulation, his or her own tendency to covet a position in the dominant group. Dialogue after the simulation was not so much on how to adapt it for use in their parishes as on their sudden realization of their own personal will to power. These men and women could speak their feelings and were honest and courageous. They were all clearly humbled by their experience within that power-class simulation.

That afternoon, as was our practice, we had a celebration of the Catholic Mass. Participants were somewhat subdued as a function of the afternoon's affective activity, but some spoke of their feelings within the framework of the prayers. At the moment before communion, however, the leader, an Irish priest, inadvertently omitted the traditional kiss of peace. Quantum thinking sees that as synchronicity. There are no accidents. The simulated division into adversarial groups during the afternoon's learning activity was a symbol of the real division among these people, a division so deeply unconscious that no one else seemed to notice the symptoms.

A Daring Improvisation

That evening I did not go to supper with them. Instead I designed a daring, improvised simulation that would directly address their present situation. At the end of their meal, I invited them to join me for a unique learning task inspired by Starpower. Everyone joined in. I described the simulated situation and asked them to do some simple learning tasks. I explained: "A new government has been elected in Zambia. It is staunchly determined to make all institutions fully Zambian. A law has been passed excluding all churchmen and women of American and European origin from Zambia. They must leave by the first of next month." I then described our two-part task.

Task A

All those who will be sent home to the United States or Europe gather in one group to decide: What will you do in the weeks remaining before you leave? How will you organize for your own personal future? You can respond to these questions on the personal level. What are your hopes for the Catholic Church in Zambia? Offer these decisions as a group.

All those whose origin is Zambian form another group to decide: What will you personally do in the next few weeks to work for the necessary reorganization of parishes, dioceses, schools, colleges, hospitals, and seminaries of the Zambian Catholic Church? What are your hopes for the future? We will carry on this dialogue in small groups for one hour and then report to the entire group before going to Task B.

Task B

Ten years later, you all meet in Rome. What do you think is happening in Zambia? What is happening for all of you who left Zambia ten years ago? Respond in the same small groups: those who have left (Europeans) and those who have stayed (Zambians). We will discuss your speculations in half an hour.

I had written out the two parts of the learning task and had given copies to each group. I sat by as an observer, a living video camera, trying to capture the immediate responses. The Zambian group, six men and six women, went at this task with gusto and lots of laughter. Indeed, their energy was so high that one had the fantastic thought that they had been anticipating this opportunity for some time. Their affect was clearly glad and a little bit scared.

The expatriate group, seven men and one woman, was subdued and confused. Their affect was clearly a mix of sad and mad. Voices were dark and murmuring. The one woman in the group kept trying to say something, but she was knitting all the while and sat at the margin of the group. She could not get the men in the group to hear her point. After a quarter of an hour, I went up to the group and pointed out to one Irish priest that Mary Anne was not "in" the group. He was surprised and said: "Oh, I see. Yes, yes, Mary Anne, what is it you want to say?" He had been entirely unconscious of her efforts toward physical and verbal inclusion. Here was another symbol of a common lack of awareness.

The Zambian group got louder and louder, with more and more laughter and shouts of "Oh, yes! For sure!" They were working in their own language and their exuberance was felt across the room. The other group became pensive and quiet as the hour came to a close. I asked, "Who wants to share your findings?"

The Zambian group fell silent, waiting for the others to speak. A tall Irishman finally confessed that they were all feeling angry and sad about the law. For many of them, the first concern was how would they sell their cars? This brought a physical sigh from the Zambian group and, I confess, a shocked expression from me. Others in the expatriate group said they were all heading to Rome to meet the papal organizers of their respective orders and would wait for the ban to be lifted, which they expected to occur soon. Another palpable sigh was heard from the Zambians. The Irish nun said she personally hoped for the best for the new Zambian church and would be cheering for them from wherever her order sent her. The men clearly did not share her optimism but said they would be ready to return to help clean things up as soon as possible. My internal video camera was working apace, trying to get as much data as possible for the entire group to consider afterward.

The Zambians all began to talk at once. There was no end to their enthusiasm for this opportunity. There would be no hierarchy, they said. There would be no more building of churches. Seminaries would be closed. Young men interested in ministry would go to work with a priest in a parish to study by using a mentoring system. Women as well as men would run village parishes. Men and women in charge of parishes would work at other jobs to make their living. No funds would be accepted from Rome. Indeed, the Zambian church would send funds to Rome for use in needy situations around the world. Schools and hospitals would be self-sustaining through tuition and fees. There would be an annual conference of all Catholics to decide policy and processes. Zambian forms and symbols would be used in the sacraments.

When an Irish Jesuit interrupted with a sharp, "Now hold on there!" a young Zambian priest turned to him with bright, angry eyes and a very sad voice. "When you were my professor in the seminary, didn't you know how you dominated us? Didn't you know how all Zambian forms and symbols were dishonored? Didn't you see how demoralized we were? How could you have been so blind?"

For the first time in my life I saw a priest cry. The Irish Jesuit came over, with great humility and tenderness, sobbing his sorrow and surprise: "Mikaeli, I swear to God, I never realized you felt like this." Soon the whole room was in tears. Simple forms of reconciliation were occurring everywhere, an embrace, a handshake, a rueful shake of the head, a smile. I raised my voice over the crowd and said, daringly, "This afternoon Father John omitted inviting us to the kiss of peace. It seems to me it is time for that now." The affective communication was profound.

After that small ceremony, I invited the two groups to set themselves to Task B. It is ten years later, and you are meeting in Rome. What's happening in Zambia? What's happening for all of you who left Zambia ten years ago? After half an hour, the speculation was exciting. The expatriates had all started working in other parts of Africa with a firm new perspective on their responsibilities to the principles of equality and cultural respect. It was obvious what they had learned. The Zambians shared their projection of hard times and new structures and emphasized their own need to avoid replicating what they had found so offensive in colonialism. They were realistic and more subdued in this projection task, but they nevertheless worked together with alacrity and hopefulness.

Can you see how these learning tasks, replete with affect and psychomotor aspects as well as significant cognitive content, moved this group of adults to intense learning?

Reflection

It was an exhausted group that left the room that night. The next day, a new tone pervaded the workshop. Tasks went on, lessons about models for transformative leadership were learned and reported, but the process was somehow cleaner, the dialogue more open and honest. When we got to reflecting further on the experience of the night before, a wise young Zambian woman said: "That story and those tasks shook up stuff in me that I never had thought of before! I was surprised how ready I was to think of it!" An old Irish missionary said the same thing: "I discovered how I really felt, what I really thought, who I really was." Okolo confided, "I learned what I do not want to be and what I must be as a pastor, as a man." Margaret Wheatley's challenge in relation to quantum thinking fits here: "Only by venturing into the unknown do we enable new ideas to take shape, and those shapes are different for each voyager" (Wheatley, 1999, p. xiv).

More than two decades have passed since this educational event in Zambia. It surely was an occasion of ontological knowing! No doubt the participants in that workshop will remember all that occurred that evening just as well or even better than I am remembering it. The event—affective, cognitive, psychomotor as it was—moved them to learn the abstract concepts of equality and mutual respect in startling new ways. Out of different cultural paradigms they responded differently, but with a unity based on nothing more than their shared humanity. With new self-respect on all sides, these men and women could build a church based on a common sense of equality.

Design Challenges

- Often we use published curriculum materials without amending them to the culture of the group. That culture can be that of children, African Americans, Hispanics, single mothers, women, churchmen, whomever. As part of our preparation we can examine printed materials in terms of the *who*—the learners. Select any printed materials you use in your program. Then consider any single, relatively homogeneous group you work with and examine that material in terms of their culture and context. How will it speak to that group?

- Based on this story, imagine a situation and a set of culturally appropriate learning tasks you could use with a single group of learners involving affective and cognitive and psychomotor activities. What do you think might happen if you used such an engaging design with the group?

- Look again at the six quantum concepts. How did you see these at work in this Zambian story?

  Relatedness: All that we do in design and teaching is related.

Holistic perspective: The whole is far more than the sum of its parts. Learners learn more than we teach!

Duality: Embrace the opposites, use "both/and" thinking (light is both a particle and a wave). Open questions invite both/and thinking and dialogue.

Uncertainty: Every theory is constantly being constructed by application to new contexts. We do not control another's learning.

Participation: The observer is part of what she observes. Each person's perception of any given reality is different, dependent on that person's context and culture. We evoke the world we perceive.

Energy: Learning demands energy.

11

Immediacy

Teaching What Is Really Useful to Learners

In Chapter One you read a brief description of immediacy. In this story immediacy of learning is seen as a vital principle that enabled this small group of community development specialists in war-torn El Salvador to grasp what they were learning with both hands. David Rogers, an energetic, thoughtful man, took over management of Save the Children's (SCF) community development program in El Salvador at a critical moment in history. Rogers invited me to conduct a training of the field staff of SCF, who worked in three or four villages in a mountain area some fifty miles outside the capital city of San Salvador.

The Situation and the Setting

Rogers' purpose for this training-of-trainers course was not only to sharpen the community education skills of the staff doctors, nurses, agriculturists, social workers, and water specialists but also to enable them to take time to examine their responses to the volatile situation in which they worked. As he put it, "I want them to have time to tell their stories, to let one another hear how they are really feeling in the midst of all this chaos." Rogers was in fact a quantum thinker. He knew that "in the quantum world, relationship is the key determiner" (Wheatley, 1999, p. 11) and that "chaos is necessary to new creative ordering" (Wheatley, 1999, p. 13).

El Salvador at the time was a tinderbox. Community development was often used to restore a community after a violent incident
had torn it apart physically and spiritually. Government military
personnel lived in nervous fear of "guerrillas"; those engaged in the
struggle for change lived in fear of the government. I spent a month
in Antigua, Guatemala, restoring my dormant Spanish and then
took the crowded bus from Antigua to San Salvador, the capital of
El Salvador.

At one point after we had crossed the border of Salvador and
Guatemala, the bus was halted by a ragtag group of soldiers who
stormed onto the old vehicle, rattling its floorboards with their
boots, their M16 automatics at the ready. My heart stopped when
they looked at me and demanded my passport. I handed it to them
and held my breath. Visions of what might happen rolled across the
screen of my imagination like a dreadful B film with me as both
heroine and victim. It was a long half-hour before they came back,
thrust the passport into my hands, and commanded the Guatemalan
and Salvadoran passengers, whom they had lined up outside, to
board the bus again. As we jolted over the dirt roads into the city,
I realized I had just completed a large part of the emotional needs
assessment for the upcoming course. This is the kind of crisis the
staff with whom I would be working experienced every day. I had
had a taste of their chaos. Little did I realize I would have an even
greater sense of their struggle before the training was over.

Designing the Program Design

The agency has a bright, well-equipped office in a residential district of San Salvador. We spent a week before the training program
working together on the design. My experience with the soldiers on
the bus, as well as the daily newspapers and radio announcements
of violence, corroborated my passion for immediacy in this design.
Since these folks and the people they served were in a daily life-
and-death situation, everything we did in the six-day workshop
must meet real needs.

Rogers is an experienced Peace Corps trainer, so he and I and the skilled training specialist on his staff, Maria Gonzales, sat together to design. I asked that we first design our designing. I wanted time in the impact area, where the staff lived and worked, to meet all the staff and see them in the field. I wanted to read all their reports and get to know their reality so that whatever we taught would have immediate usefulness to them in this critical situation. Only then could we accountably sit down with our seven steps of design to write a draft of the program. I hoped we could have one or two of the field staff work with us on this program.

Any educator goes into a situation with a boilerplate of concepts, skills, and attitudes he or she either wants to teach or can teach. A dialogue approach to adult learning does not deny this or judge it as wrong. The operative word is *dialogue*. These people had called me to El Salvador to teach them what I knew. I knew I could not do that with accountability if I did not first find out what they knew, what their lives were like, how they thought about their work, what they perceived they still needed to learn. Although this dialogue would take place within the two-week training session in a set of learning tasks, some of it had to take place before we even began to design the session.

There is a strange paradox I have observed: the more structure there is, the greater chance of spontaneity. Quantum thinking recognizes the universe as a self-regulating system where spontaneity is part of the intrinsic order. I remembered an experience I had with a famous psychologist who held a week-long workshop in the Adirondack Mountains. I attended with great expectation of what I would learn. The first day, however, the 120 participants heard this old man say: "Decide what you want to learn and tell us. As soon as you are ready we shall teach." It was not a happy two days for me. One hundred twenty men and women cannot design a curriculum for a week's study from a blank page. I soon realized I had to leave. When I told the learned doctor my plans, he admonished me: "Oh, stay! It is so interesting. It will all come out all right." That was not

quantum thinking; that felt like manipulation. I did not see El Salvador as a research laboratory for discovering the effectiveness of
innovative learning styles.

The difference between what Paulo Freire calls the "banking system" and what he calls "dialogue" is respect for the learners and
their immediate needs (Freire , 1972, p. 67). Dialogue education is
never an adversarial situation. This dialogue approach is a structured partnership for listening and learning, with clearly delineated
roles.

Field Visit

Maria Gonzales and I went off to the impact area where Save the
Children has its programs. We met the community development
specialists, among them Carlos Castillo, the field coordinator who
organized community efforts in two separate geographical areas. We
saw the two public health doctors and four nurses who were engaged
in a huge vaccination program. We met the two agriculturists who
worked with farmers and the water specialist who was working with
the local government to set up a sanitation system. Local women
were secretaries and file clerks in the impact area office and two
young men, recent graduates of the local high school, were working as health aides to the public health team.

Castillo and two other field staff were old friends of mine from
the international training session held at SCF headquarters in Westport, Connecticut, so I did not have to start from scratch to build a
relationship with them. My struggle with Spanish offered opportunities for lots of laughter, and I knew that laughter would be a useful resource. My immediate needs in terms of language, as well as
my obvious effort to learn, reversed the roles of teacher and student
beautifully. They would be my guides, my teachers, as I rebuilt this
elusive language skill. In every non–English-speaking country where
I have worked, my very desire to learn the language created a relationship with the local people and my struggling efforts created occasions for hilarity. As we saw in Chapter Six, the power of this

relationship between teacher and student is ineffable. Language, even at its most stuttering, can be a great help in building that relationship. Gonzales is fluent in English and served me well as translator. She, too, was conscious that my faulty Spanish evoked the help of the staff, and she wisely kept in the background when she could.

Perhaps nowhere else in the world of education is the power of the backseat driver felt as in adult learning. This backseat driver is a quiet resource who is there to be called on, unobtrusive, and safe. Since adults learn by doing, we must design opportunities for that doing, using new knowledge, skills, and attitudes. But the learners have to do it. It is the learners who have the immediate need to practice the skills and attitudes and work with the new concepts. We have to learn to take a backseat gracefully. Just being there is not an easy role for the traditional lectern professor. Gonzales gave me a great example of how to do this well. She would prove herself even more skillful as we developed and led the program.

We visited clinics, schools, and farms. We chatted with village leaders, priests, teachers, and wives. We played with endless numbers of beautiful, brown-eyed babies, their mothers' eyes shining with pride as I praised the beauty of each one. Again I saw how basic human courtesy, expressed in respect for each individual and for the cultural practices, is such a profound instrument for learning. I was learning because they respected me. They were learning through my respect. Under the umbrella of respect, learning is always mutual and immediate.

I did not, of course, write down a word while I was with the staff in the field. Once alone in the hotel room, however, I wrote masses of questions and brought them to Rogers and Gonzales. It was vital for me, not to understand everything but to have the right questions. Dialogue education—in this case in an El Salvadoran mountain village—is a mirror held up to nature. I have always held that my motto, as teacher, must be, *Pray for doubt!* I hoped that the learners would take the same attitude. Rogers and Gonzales were learning, too. The more questions I asked, the more they probed their own efforts with the field staff, standing back to get the whole picture. This was a holistic, quantum approach.

We had a three-hour meeting of the whole field staff there at which I asked: "What do you wish to happen during this two-week educational event?" I asked them to talk first in arbitrary groups of three, not grouped by the various disciplines, such as health or agriculture. We asked them whether we might tape this dialogue so that we could use it for our design of learning tasks when we went back to San Salvador.

As described in the story in Ethiopia in Chapter Four, doing an educational needs assessment involves three actions: observe, study, ask. The field staff had read a draft outline of what we might do during the two-week training. They knew from their three colleagues what we had emphasized in the international staff training these three had attended in Westport. They also knew that they had a consultative voice here. They were offering suggestions as to what they wanted and needed. It was our role, Rogers' and Gonzales' and mine, to take these suggestions and decide what we could do in the allotted time. We had the deliberative voice. Thirty people cannot make such a design for staff training. The quality of the dialogue assured them that their suggestions would be honored and implemented, as far as possible, in the name of immediacy.

The Program and the Process

The educational event had already begun with my visit to the field. There is an immediacy in such an educational learning needs and resources assessment in beginning the dialogue. As the wife of Arthur Miller's agonized protagonist in *The Death of a Salesman* tells us: "Attention must be paid!" What we were doing in this two-day visit prior to designing the program was paying attention, using the model that emphasizes listening, respect, dialogue, immediacy, attention to people's experience, engagement, and honoring people as subjects of their own life and of their own education—all the qualities of dialogue education.

Rogers made the popular decision that Castillo, the field coordinator, would join us in the four-day design session in San Salvador. The field staff expressed their gratitude at having been heard and sent Castillo off with us, knowing the dialogue would continue. The design process is a central part of an educational event. Gonzales, Rogers, Castillo, and I worked for four days, using the seven steps of design, struggling with sequence, setting learning tasks, and making materials.

A delightful aspect of this workshop, which has been consistent in every educational event I have been involved in throughout Central America, is that dancing was a given. Indeed, the payment of the local band was in the training budget. We would work hard in that long training session. Each evening the tables and chairs were pushed back, the bandstand was set up, and the room became a fiesta ballroom. Here was real immediacy. The field staff appeared not to be tired after a night of dancing. In fact they worked even harder the next day. Personally, I adore the custom. If there is one educational practice I would insistently urge on readers, it is this one: dance!

The Seven Steps of Design

After reading the transcriptions from the audiotape of the meeting with the field staff, the design team worked out these Seven Steps.

Who

The participants were the two community development specialists who organized efforts in two separate geographical areas, the two public health doctors and four nurses doing a huge vaccination program, the two agriculturists who worked with farmers, the water specialist who was working with the local government to set up a sanitation system, the two local women who were secretaries and file clerks in the impact area office, and the two young men who were working as health aides to the public health team. The entire field staff, along with Gonzales and Castillo, would be present—sixteen men and women from all parts of El Salvador.

What about other local people with whom they worked closely? These people could not spend six days in such a course. Unless someone was prepared to spend the entire time doing the workshop, they could not be included. I call this *comprehensive participation*. I insisted on it for two reasons: when a new person joins a group, it becomes a new group; also, the cultural changes that could be effected by this kind of education would be vitiated by someone not taking part fully in the decision to make such changes. Since Rogers had duties in San Salvador that would involve him on many of the six days of the workshop, he wisely decided not to take part, honoring this principle of comprehensive participation. This is a difficult principle to honor when working with very busy people. Consider making the entire time shorter in order to welcome people who cannot attend a longer session.

The number of participants is a vital variable for a program's success. Sixteen was just right for this group. With that number we could go deep into issues, take time for dialogue, practice skills, build a bond of new friendship, and make decisions with complete participation. I was to be facilitator. Gonzales, as my assistant, would set each of the learning tasks. This was to honor my clumsy Spanish and help me in understanding the responses to each task.

Why

The present situation *why* is the situation that calls for the training event. These staff people were challenged by a tough professional enterprise: reaching vast numbers of peasants in their rural impact area with new skills, knowledge, and attitudes for their own development in a context of terror and war. They needed enhanced skills for this task.

The outcome *why* is that they will be able to use new skills and new theories to do their community education more effectively. Note that the outcome, being general, does not indicate what is to

happen during the six days. That specificity is the work of achievement based objectives.

Where

The immediate issue of safety arose as we decided on the site of the
training. The agency could bring the entire field staff into San Salvador and then do the training in a center in the city. Neither I nor
the field staff wanted that. Staff did not want to leave their families
in the immediate danger of the volatile political situation, and I
wanted them close to their work sites for practical work.

The danger that a gathering such as this training workshop
might be seen by the military with suspicion had to be faced. Rogers
and Castillo spent long hours with the local soldiers, explaining our
purpose and getting the necessary permits for the event. This
seemed unusual to me but not to them. They faced this kind of
minor crisis every day in their work. The immediacy of safety in the
learning situation struck me.

We would work in a church hall adjacent to the agency office.
It had a kitchen so we could make lunch for all the field staff, and
the secretaries could check the office for messages at intervals. The
hall was well lighted. It faced a busy street, however, so we had to
deal with a variety of youngsters watching events through the open
windows, as well as the loud street noises made by ancient, unmuf-
fled trucks and taxis. Practical work would be done by sector staff
in the clinics and on one of the farms where they usually work. The
locus of control is deeply related to the site of an educational event.
If it is vital to control the number of participants in order to have
accountable adult learning, it is also essential to control the site.
Imagine the difference if this field staff education had taken place
at a hotel meeting room in San Salvador. Consider who was in control in the church hall of this little mountain town. Who would
have been in control in a San Salvador hotel?

Perhaps the principle of immediacy can help us in such decisions. How close to the work site can we get to do the education

and training? This is not only for the advantage of practical application but also to ensure that the locus of control is shared by learners.

When

We all agreed that six days was the maximum we could ask people to be away from their immediate responsibilities, but it was the minimum in which we could effect the kinds of learning and change needed. The hours of work and meals and dancing were left to Castillo with reference to the needs of field staff to be with their families in the town. We agreed that we would work for thirty-six hours: six hours a day for six days. This gave us a framework into which we could design learning tasks.

What

The *what* were the skills, knowledge, and attitudes that we felt would meet the immediate needs and wants of the field staff. Notice that these skills, knowledge, and attitudes are nouns whereas the *what for* (achievement based objectives; see next) begin with verbs. The content was

- The current five-year plan

- Our recent achievements

- How to give and get feedback

- Basic adult learning theories

- The difference between monologue and dialogue

- Communication skills

- Situations they have been involved in because of the war

- The difference between deliberative and consultative voices

- Time management skills

- How to have an effective meeting

Again, we knew we would be dealing with much more than what was on this list as we met for six days in that dusty church hall. This was to give us a framework for our efforts—a framework, not a boundary.

What For

We then worked to set achievement based objectives that would enable us to meet the needs and wants of the field staff and be accountable to them. By *accountable* I mean that we do what we say we will do. The structure for accountability involves these objectives *(what for)* and the learning tasks *(how)*.

In this case, we set up the following achievement based objectives. *By the end of the six days, all sixteen participants will have*

- Described their sector efforts (health, agriculture, and so on)

- Identified some major problems facing them

- Reviewed the current five-year plan

- Examined situations they have been involved in because of the war

- Reviewed basic adult learning theories at work in their community education efforts

- Distinguished between monologue and dialogue

- Practiced communication skills

- Designed community education sessions for their sector by using dialogue instead of monologue

- Designed problem-posing learning materials: songs, stories, drama, pictures

- Practiced teaching in the impact area by using their designs

- Received comments on their designs and their practice teaching

- Examined a set of guidelines on how to hold effective meetings

- Celebrated their achievements as field staff in this program

We knew that these objectives would not be the only things done in this six-day event. They provide the framework for the learning tasks. As achievement based objectives, they indicate what the learners are going to accomplish during the allotted time and guide in the design of learning tasks. They are the structure, not the boundaries, of the event. The form of these objectives is significant. They constitute an accountable contract between teacher and learners. It promises that learners will have accomplished all this by the end of the course. This form of learning objective is based on research showing how adults learn cognitive, affective, and psycho-motor lessons by doing them. These objectives demonstrate that the teacher is accountable to the learners as well as the other way around. Accountability is mutual. Achievement based objectives assure participants that by the end of the session they will know they know. How do they know they know? They just did it (Vella, 1998).

How

This step (how) is the set of learning tasks for the group of sixteen field staff. More than anything, I wanted to model a dialogue approach. These people had been taught by monologue in school, uni-

versity, church, and government. By using learning tasks and learning materials designed for dialogue, with immediate usefulness to
their jobs, we might stir in them the desire to use such dialogue
in their own teaching.

In all of this, I was aware of the danger of cultural intrusiveness—
of insensitivity to time-honored rites and customs. I trusted that I
could be a backseat driver who would often have a consultative, not
a deliberative, voice. Since it was all occurring in Spanish, my lin-
guistic disadvantage was actually a distinct cultural advantage.

Dialogue education is a means to political action: changing the
social paradigms. One demonstrates the inadequacies of the old paradigm in an effort to lead people out of it into a new pattern of
thinking or doing. As we move from a mechanistic to a quantum
view of the world, we honor the difficulty of this change. Political
action such as this often takes place on the microlevel: a shift of the
locus of control when the learner says to herself, "I will decide thus
and so." Affirmation of such a decision is one of the major roles of
the teacher of adult learners.

The seven steps of design seem tightly linear as we describe
them. If you could have heard the rambling, circular, dancing
thoughts and dreams evoked in that little design group by these
questions—*Who? Why? What? What for? When? Where? How?*—you
would see that this structure is itself an opportunity for listening to
one another's spontaneity—an opportunity for dialogue and quantum thinking. We found these seven steps a valid tool to focus the
plan on the learners' immediate needs.

On the first day of this training-of-trainers workshop there were
no lectures. The learning tasks were all inductive—inviting people
to draw from their experiences, tell their stories, understand their
life and work. When Gonzales read the summary chart of the research of Malcolm Knowles about adult learning, it was presented as
a touchstone against which to measure the factors staff had already

mentioned from their own analysis. All research was presented as an open system that might be questioned, argued, or edited to apply more immediately to this cultural context. While they were editing, arguing, and questioning, they were learning and re-creating the content for their unique context.

This is what we mean by dialogue education. Every piece of theory is a hypothesis to be tested again and again in new contexts. This is surely the most scientific of scientific methods—and sound quantum thinking. If a theory does not work in a certain context, is it the context that is wrong? In a quantum perspective, the context is definitive. In a dialogue approach we present sound content through learning tasks to see how that content can apply in a specific cultural context.

People ask me all the time, "How do you use a dialogue approach when teaching hard data?" I suggest that you present whatever content you are teaching as an open system and invite adult learners to question, argue, and edit in the light of their own life experience. Thus is theory developed, thus are paradigm shifts catalyzed, thus are adult learners taught as subjects of their own learning. This is quantum theory at its best: *we evoke the world we perceive*. In the design challenges that follow this story, there will be opportunities to design learning tasks by using data in such a way as to evoke immediate response and learning.

Immediacy in Danger

The perils of war-torn El Salvador, which had been described all too poignantly by the staff on the first day of the workshop, were felt by all of us on the fifth day. We were quite exhausted, having worked all day and danced long into the night, designed and created learning materials, taught in the field, and worked on feedback. Before starting their second designs, the field staff suggested an outing to the family farm of one of the staff. We packed a picnic lunch and set out to explore Castillo's brother's farm, walk in the fresh air, and take a long lunch break.

Castillo was showing me some of the operations of the farm when his face suddenly turned white with fear. I turned around to see a great mass of M16 rifles pointing at us all. The soldiers had apparently arisen from behind piles of hay. There were at least thirty of them, all heavily armed with M16s, grenades, and side pistols. I stood there trembling like a child. One of my best friends, Maura Clarke, a Maryknoll Sister, had died with three colleagues in El Salvador at the hands of military men not many years before. Just the thought of it brought tears to my eyes.

Much discussion in rather loud Spanish got us as far as identifying ourselves as staff of a community development agency. None of us had any official identification with us on this picnic. I was one of the major problems: How did they know I was not an American infiltrator? In my dusty slacks and sweater I could have passed for any kind of spy. My trembling did not help much, and I lost all touch with whatever Spanish skills I had been so proudly developing through the workshop.

My passport lay safely in my briefcase locked in the field office. "For safekeeping," Castillo had said. Right now I wanted safekeeping for all of us, not for the passport. We were corralled toward the road where a radio set was crackling. The young commander of these government troops told us he would check us out with the high command in a neighboring town. It was a harrowing half-hour. Later I could look back on it as a great learning experience, feeling what these people felt every day, but at the time I could not appreciate any aspect of it. All I could feel was fear and trembling. No abstraction meant anything to me at that point. All that I wanted was the immediacy of a safe conduct back to town. Prayers and deep breathing sustained us during that silent half-hour. Where were the dancing, laughing Salvadorans and the humor-loving facilitator? We were learning together how vulnerable and frightened we all really are.

Finally, a thirty-minute eternity later, the radio sparked into life. Gruff voices were heard from afar and the commander turned to wave us into our pickup truck. We drove off in deep silence. There were no jokes, no laughter, no comments. They knew better than I the dire possibilities of that experience. I thought of Maura and her friends and realized how grateful I was to be alive.

The learning mood of the group deepened after this event. Nothing was said about it. They could not speak about it for safety reasons. The distance between us, however, instead of widening, narrowed. I realized that although I would go back to the United States and relative safety, the moment of vulnerability we shared would never go away. We were bound now by cords of remembered fear and fulfilled hope. The pain of war-torn El Salvador would always be immediate to me. The band came as scheduled that evening, and we danced with a somewhat heightened *joie de vivre*.

Training staff in the United States later asked why I had not used that event as a pregnant story to analyze field staff's feelings (and mine) about the dangers in which they worked and lived. I was reminded of a phrase I often use when guiding students in the writing of case studies or stories that teach: the materials you use must be close enough to be immediate, distant enough to be safe! Until today, this event has not been distant enough for me to describe.

Evaluation

Months and years after that six-day training, Rogers reported examples of the staff's depth and insightful decision making in that impact area. They continued to use the seven steps in their design of training in health, agriculture, and community leadership. We know that political action is an indirect result of education. Education can lead to the transformation of those who will then transform the society through political action. El Salvador, like so many war-torn countries, needs men and women strong and sure in their values, knowledge, and skills to effect healthy political transformation. The immediacy of this educational objective is global.

Design Challenges

- What changes would you propose in the design of this El Salvador training-of-trainers workshop if you were involved in it today? Why?

- What else should I have known before starting the training workshop in El Salvador? What would have had more immediate usefulness to me and the field staff during that first week?

- Suppose you are designing a training program for managers in communication skills. You want to teach the concepts and skills of open and closed communications. How can you present that theory as an open system, inviting questions, arguments, and editing by the adult learners? What is the advantage to you as teacher—and to them as learners—of using dialogue education?

- Take any educational event you have designed. Consider what the content is: the skills, knowledge, or attitudes you are teaching. How could you have presented that content as an open system, inviting questions, arguments, and editing?

- After all this, what does immediacy mean to you? Why do you consider it vital in designing adult learning events?

12

Assuming New Roles for Dialogue
Embracing the Death of the Professor

Paulo Freire once said to me in conversation: "Only the student can name the moment of the death of the professor." You read that phrase in Chapter One as you examined the importance of clear roles in an adult learning situation. This story focuses on the role of the "professor" and the transformation of that role demanded by dialogue education. In the Maryknoll Graduate School of Theology in Westchester County, New York, a group of earnest educators were seriously examining their roles. They had long been perplexed by the distance between the world of academia and the vibrant reality faced by graduates as they entered their ministry. This ministry included intense cross-cultural situations in the United States and international settings. Whatever these professors were teaching—scripture, sociology, history, theology, art, physics, political science—it needed to be taught in a way that prepared these young people for the complex reality of their ministry.

The Context

All of these professors had read Freire's *Pedagogy of the Oppressed* (1972), and all wanted to incorporate a dialogue approach into their way of teaching. They simply did not know how to begin. I had been invited to lead a short course in dialogue education with Maryknoll lay missionaries each spring. These men and women—professionals in law, medicine, nursing, education, and business—responded en-thusiastically to that course, which gave them practical methods for teaching in the rural or urban developing world situations to which they were heading.

Professors from the Maryknoll Graduate School of Theology also taught short courses and workshops for the lay folk in this curricu-lum. After having studied the principles and practices of the dia-logue approach, however, the lay missionaries became quite critical of the more formal methods used by the professors. Why weren't they using adult education approaches when teaching their courses? As one professor wisely noted: "We must either study this dialogue method with Jane or put her course at the end of their curriculum to avoid comparison!"

The Learners

Invitations were sent out to all the professors in the Maryknoll Graduate School of Theology and to all the professors from other universities who taught in the lay missionary program. We proposed a three-day workshop to give professors time to reflect upon new re-search in adult learning, design a section of their own course via this approach, and share that design with colleagues for feedback. This would be done at the graduate school in a formal classroom setting. This was their milieu. I wanted to demonstrate how it could come alive and become a place for learning comparable to the aban-doned cowshed in Nepal or the noisy church hall in El Salvador. Modeling an approach to learning means being true to it in all cir-cumstances. This was an excellent opportunity to prove that the principles of dialogue learning do not depend on the environment, the operator factor, or the topic being taught. Here was a chance to test, under very real circumstances, the entire hypothesis. If it could work with this group of professors and university faculty in a grad-uate classroom, it might just be worth further examination.

We actually did this workshop twice for over twenty faculty members from this graduate school and other universities. I was delighted to have Richard Schaull of Princeton in the group. He had written the foreword to the 1972 edition of *Pedagogy of the Oppressed*. In that foreword he said: "The development of an educational methodology that facilitates the 'practice of freedom' by which men and women deal critically and creatively with reality and discover how to participate in the transformation of their world will inevitably lead to tension and conflict within our society. But it could also contribute to the formation of a new man and mark the beginning of a new era in Western history."

Schaull came to this course with three colleagues from Latin America to discover practical ways to implement the radical theory he had written about in that foreword. There were scholars of many disciplines in the room and many years of teaching experience. All had at least one Ph.D. and many came bedecked with honors from publishing, research, or teaching. The very fact that they gave their time to this endeavor demonstrated their openness and humility. Deans and administrators joined teaching faculty. There were men and women, priests and ministers, nuns and mothers. It was a diverse and formidable group.

It struck me that all of these people had gone through graduate school themselves. They had paid all the dues needed to complete their dissertations and win their teaching and research wings. It was not surprising that they internalized the methods of those graduate schools. We teach the way we have been taught. They had all experienced the modeling of traditional, didactic, graduate school methods described by Freire as "banking" and described by me as "monologue." What could a three-day workshop change in their skills and knowledge and especially in their attitude toward learning and the learners?

I had the opportunity to speak recently with an engineer at NASA who asked incredulously: "What has quantum theory got to do with education? Are you looking at it as a metaphor or something?" I see this graduate school experience with new eyes now as I look at it through the lens of quantum theory. I was inviting these men and women to change not a technique but their whole way of looking at the world, at relationships, at the content they taught, at themselves. Their skepticism and resistance was understandable. They were asked to enter a behavioral revolution. This was no metaphor.

These men and women would certainly be subjects in the learning experience. They would decide what, if anything, of this approach they could use in their graduate courses. We built that choice into the design by inviting them to select one of their courses, use this approach to design a part of it, and then share that design with their colleagues. We began the workshop, modeling the dialogue approach in the set learning tasks, inviting first their reflection on the objectives and the program. I explained how these objectives had been informed by the needs assessment interviews we had completed prior to the course. I invited them to review the achievement based objectives for the three-day workshop: *By the end of this three-day workshop, all participants will have*

- Reviewed current adult learning theories

- Assessed their own courses for learner engagement and accountability

- Distinguished between the "banking" and the dialogue approach to learning and teaching (monologue and dialogue)

- Used case studies, critical incidents, open questions, charts, found objects, stories, lectures, mnemonic devices, sociodrama, video, seminars, models, web charts, snow cards, and a gallery walk in a dialogue mode

- Designed a section of a course using this dialogue approach

- Designed learning tasks and materials for that course

- Shared their designs with their peers for feedback

- Named future opportunities for studying this dialogue approach to graduate education

The Program and the Process

I then showed them the program I had designed to achieve these objectives. The program was a set of learning tasks that they would do in small learning teams. One of the learning tasks was entitled, "Expectations, Task 2: in groups of three, name your hopes and fears about this three-day workshop." Their responses were significant. A professor of scripture was diffident and concerned: How could he cover the immense amount of material that he had to teach if he used such a dialogue approach? The ethics professor was skeptical: How can students be invited to make judgments as subjects before they have learned the rules? The political science team, including Richard Schaull, was concerned about equal time for each of their specialties: law, international economics, and sociology. How could they be ensured time for teaching all that they had to teach if they used this dialogue approach?

Then came their list of hopes and fears for the workshop. They wanted to learn new techniques, learn new methods and practice them, learn how to motivate students to learn, learn how to ensure adequate time to cover their material. They asked: How can we be sure learners know what they need to know? How serious is this method? How appropriate for graduate school is this method? How much can we do in a three-day workshop? These hopes and fears are classic. I have seen similar concerns from field staff in international settings and from social workers and nurses in urban U.S. community health clinics. With our own experience in graduate school coloring our perceptions, we find it hard to give up the idea that education is merely a sharing of facts and concepts. In the abstract, all these professors knew that effective education involved all three aspects: cognitive, affective, and psychomotor. We all are hungry for a sound, empirically based approach to the teaching-learning process that allows us to assure learners that they really know what they came to learn. We call this *accountability*. We are all terrified, however, at the change in our role such a new approach might demand.

Each learning task in the three-day workshop invited them to practice dialogue with one another and with the resources that went with the task. These resources included written material from textbooks and articles, a lecture that I offered, a video, clips from a film, a clip from an audiotape, a case study. The difference here was that their role as learners was now an active role; they had to do something in small groups with these resources, responding to the open questions that shaped the learning tasks. They began to see the resources as learning tools, similar to the development tools named by field staff in Nepal (Chapter Nine). They began to recognize that the transformation of their role—from professor (or teller) in the banking approach to colearner and resource person in this dialogue approach—was not as threatening as they had expected.

They discovered that the sequence of learning tasks was of vital importance. We moved from description of a situation to input from research to application to our own lives and then to integration of that learning into their own lives (Vella 2000, p. 34). We used the four open questions to ensure that sequence. For example, before using a clip from the popular film *Dead Poets Society*, I set these four open questions:

1. What do you see happening here?

2. Why do you think it happens?

3. When it happens in your situation, what problems does it cause?

4. What could have been done differently to prevent what happened?

The dialogue among these professors demonstrated the engagement they wanted from their own students. They were clearly learning much from one another. They had created a context of dialogue.

Today I would share with them the research on learning from Danah Zohar and her husband, I. N. Marshall (Zohar, 1997; Zohar and Marshall, 1990). These professors had, at their lecterns, often invited graduate students to use the neural tracts of their brains to do what Zohar named serial thinking. Dialogue invites the use of neural networks and the network of networks that is the whole brain—what Zohar calls parallel and then quantum thinking. Learning tasks as they are used in this dialogue approach always invite parallel or quantum thinking through the application and integration sections of the task (Vella, 2000, p. 33). Without using the language of the recent research, we were nonetheless practicing the concepts and skills of quantum learning.

Quantum physics gives new weight to context, relationship, personal perception, holistic viewpoint, fluidity of fact and content, and the celebration of opposites. Zohar reminds us: a quantum entity must always be seen within the larger context of its defining relationships. Change the context and the entity itself is different (Zohar, 1997, p. 46). As these professors examined an alternative to their classic role in these three short days, they realized the hard work that faced them: to consider using needs assessment, learning tasks, the seven steps of design, and specific achievement based objectives in lieu of general outcomes. They faced building a new relationship to both their content and the graduate students they taught. They were invited to take a quantum leap into a chaotic and orderly universe and reflect both that intrinsic order and spontaneity in their courses.

Richard Schaull, confidant of Paulo Freire, said at the end of his three-day session: "I knew dialogue was important as a concept. I never knew how difficult and demanding it was as a learning tool."

The role of each of these professors now is researcher, designer, learner—with the graduate students they serve. They do not have to die when the student "names the moment of the death of the professor." They have to do something much more difficult. They have to live and learn.

Evaluation

All the professors were intense and enthusiastic in their participation in the small-group and large-group work. They were all pleased with the format and the classroom setting, since it corresponded to their normal patterns. All remarked on the obvious need in this approach for preparation time, not only for researching the content but also for designing the learning tasks. They also were able to cite the personal advantages of taking such time for preparation: the development of their own creativity, their assurance that the process was adequately structured for their own safety, and the development of models for use with other groups.

All indicated fear that they would revert to "banking" or monologue because they simply did not have enough time for planning. The revised course designs they produced during the workshop were clear indicators of their learning. As they shared these new designs with their colleagues, they often fell back into monologue. Their new skill was to recognize when such monologue occurred. Most had the good grace to laugh at themselves.

Here is a small sample of these designs to demonstrate how quickly and comprehensively these professors internalized the meaning of dialogue. Schaull's group offered an interdisciplinary module: "Knowing Oppression and Searching Our Resources for Liberation." This had been done as separate modules in the past. The three professors—sociologist, economist, anthropologist—decided to work together in designing and facilitating a single, longer module that would show the integration of all three concepts. They laid out the beginnings of the module, designing learning tasks that demonstrated their concern for safety, learners as subjects, and an inductive approach. The most significant aspect of this design was the excitement of the three team members at working together. When had sociology, economics, and anthropology collaborated before? They discovered their own expectations, fears, knowledge, and resources and therefore used these more effectively in their teaching. They had done quantum thinking to design this holistic lesson.

The New Testament scholar presented his design: "The Meaning of Ministry." The professor invited small groups, through specific learning tasks, to evoke their own experience with the New Testament. This preparatory activity was designed to motivate learners to demand new insights and the cutting edge of research on familiar texts from the professor as a resource. The professor offered new information in response to questions evoked in the first learning task. In his responses he was creating a dialogue. He had prepared charts and handouts synthesizing and summarizing this new information so he could "cover" his material. This had been his primary concern at the outset of our three-day workshop. He demonstrated how one can use this dialogue, engage the learners, motivate them to think critically, and thus teach the established curriculum.

This short workshop experience not only offered these professors a new model for their work. It also gave them an opportunity to demonstrate that they could indeed use the new model. They worked together to design a dialogue session, led a section of that session with us to demonstrate new teaching skills, received constructive feedback, and therefore gained confirmation of their ability to use this approach. How did they know they knew? They just did it (Vella, 1998)!

It was clear to all involved that one three-day workshop does not create an educational revolution. Since they were all familiar with the theory through their reading, however, they were able to anticipate further skills development as they practiced this approach. All asked for a second workshop to review their designs and deal with the results of using this approach in their respective graduate schools.

There was one significant danger they all cited: graduate school students expected the "banking" approach. We named the obvious need for safety among students and professors and for manifest evidence of the accountability of the curriculum and the teacher. Their own designs showed how cost-effective of learners' time and energy dialogue-based designs could be. This advantage had to be communicated to resistant learners. We emphasized that participation does not exclude personal responsibility. Working in a small group and working in solitude are two wheels of the cycle of learning. Celebrate the opposites. Both are vital to developing not only the concepts, skills, and attitudes being taught but also personal and social skills.

The professors recognized how their role might change when they used this dialogue approach instead of "banking." They named new activities that would be theirs: listening, observing, designing and using open questions, designing learning tasks, creating synthesis and summary papers that showed the cutting edge of research, facilitating group work, counseling resistant students, and setting personal tasks with individual learners. They might, through hard work and study, be able to name the moment of their own death as professor and celebrate their living as learners.

Design Challenges

- If you decide to use some of these intertwined principles of dialogue education in your own educational programs, how will your accustomed role change? What safety measures can you build into the design to protect your vulnerability in this new role?

- How does the scale of educational programs—the usual number of students in a class—affect your perception of your own role as professor in using a dialogue approach? What can you do to establish a relationship, one that recognizes learners as subjects of their own learning, when you face a class of fifty or sixty students? How can using small groups serve you in such a situation?

- What are the personal signs that you might be reverting to the role of the monologue-professor? Who can help you recognize these signs and guide you to a more effective new role?

- How does the quantum concept of participation help us comprehend the various perspectives we meet in students and colleagues? What use is it to you to recognize that we evoke the world we perceive?

13

Teamwork
Celebrating Learning Together

Teamwork is a principle of adult learning as well as an effective practice. You read about teamwork in Chapter One and in many of the previous stories. In this story we will see how this principle worked for Tainie Mudondo and her comrades in Zimbabwe. This landlocked nation suffered a bloody civil war before a coalition government was set up. This story shows how learning and teaching teams were used in the education of literacy coordinators in the national literacy campaign of Zimbabwe after independence.

The Situation and the Setting

Tainie Mudondo, one of the literacy coordinators, was a high school student when the call came for Zimbabweans to join Robert Mugabe in the early 1970s in a guerrilla army that would move the struggle for independence into the forests and mountains. She told me of the day she heard the call. Every single boy and girl in her high school class, she said, left their books on the desks and went off to the designated center, where they began their transformation from high school students to guerrilla soldiers.

Ms. Mudondo spent seven years in that army. She met and married her husband there and they had their first child. She went from being a raw, young, frightened recruit to being the education director of the army of liberation. She spent much of her time in the guerrilla army organizing literacy and public health courses for the young soldiers. After independence, she was demobilized into a confused Zimbabwean society with her husband and young son. There was a scramble for jobs in the large, modern city of Harare.

A letter from a colleague in Zimbabwe brought me the unexpected invitation to become part of the team that would design a national literacy campaign for Zimbabwe. This was an invitation I could not refuse. After having spent twenty-three years teaching in Tanzania, during their ongoing struggle for social, political, and economic development, I was still deeply engaged in Africa. This invitation was from the minister of education, Dzingai Mutumbuku, who had heard through my colleague, Janice McLoughlin, of my work in literacy in Tanzania. Dr. Mutumbuku invited me to join their team to design and implement a national literacy campaign by using the army of young men and women recently demobilized from the liberation forces as literacy teachers. I would be expected to train them as trainers of local village literacy coordinators.

The Ministry of Education was deeply engaged in the thousand and one political problems of the moment. At the bottom of the list lay the issue of the literacy campaign. Although my skills and advice were needed, they would be welcome only when asked for. I had had a similar role as a consultant from the University of Dar es Salaam to the Ministry of Education in Tanzania, so I had good experience in waiting. I learned at this time one of the most useful conceptual distinctions I had ever heard: a consultant has a consultative voice, that is, you can make suggestions; the members of the ministry team have a deliberative voice, that is, they make the decisions.

Once I got this distinction clear, I could relax, make my suggestions, and wait. I was introduced to Ms. Mudondo one afternoon in a town square in Harare. Tainie Mudondo (pronounced "Tiny") is just that: ninety pounds of intelligent, charming, fun-loving lady with a flair for telling stories and a passionate devotion to her family. I spent much time with Ms. Mudondo, learning her history in the army and the history of modern Zimbabwe that her story reflected.

The Learners

The ministry knew that their first advertisement for literacy coordinators would bring a flood of applications from former soldiers in the guerrilla army. These young people did not have jobs, nor did they have easy access to places at the colleges or university. It had been less than a year since independence. It would be politically dangerous to invite them to begin a program that was not ready for them. Who decides? This was another critical organizational question for the literacy campaign. Zimbabwe as a developing nation was inspired by reports of the successful Nicaraguan literacy crusade. Zimbabweans wanted to emulate much of what they were reading about that program. But that Central American nation was considerably smaller than the massive landlocked Zimbabwe. A church-based organization, the Adult Literacy Organization of Zimbabwe (ALOZ), had been doing literacy work in Zimbabwe for more than twenty years. Would ALOZ, without a political ideology and with a history of white supervision, be invited to be part of the team? Or would the ministry demand that we start from scratch?

Oliver and Gershman (1989, p. 43) remind us: "the observer is part of what she observes." The quantum concept of participation shows that we do evoke the world we perceive. I was on the Zimbabwean team just by being there, affecting the decisions without making them. My work with Ms. Mudondo continued as we learned together about literacy and about Zimbabwe, preparing ourselves to design and lead a useful training program. Finally, a decision was made at the upper levels of the Ministry of Education. We would proceed. A team of writers, to which I would be a consultant, would start designing materials for the training workshop for literacy coordinators that would be held in Harare in two months. Materials for the literacy campaign itself would be prepared by another team and sent to the training team. We would have members from ALOZ on the design team for training. We would not use their literacy materials, however, because they were not deemed politically appropriate for this moment in the history of this young nation.

Before I could teach others how to form a literacy team, I had to learn how to work in one. In this case, my professional soul screamed in frustration at the fragmentation of preparation efforts. Such fragmentation violated every principle of integrated program development. I called on my newfound awareness of my role as consultant with a consultative voice and discovered the necessary joy of detachment. I offered my opinion, gave my suggestions, and waited. This sounds easier than it was. As a member of this team, I was being asked to feel something of what these young people had felt under military discipline for seven years. "Yes, sir; no, sir; no excuse, sir!" Their membership in the guerrilla teams that had eventually won the war for independence had demanded that they do what they were told. This was what I had to do on this design team. I confess it was very difficult for me.

We met regularly under the direction of a young man named by the minister of education to head the task force for designing training. This young fellow also headed the materials development team, so we were linked at that point. Ms. Mudondo was on the ministry's payroll as a teacher assigned to design the training program. She was a vital link to the former soldiers whom we would be teaching, since she was one of them.

Teams Are the Real World

Complicating the political scene at the time was that the people of the southern part of the new Zimbabwe were not in agreement with those around Harare and in the north. This strong cleft in loyalty and political perspective was reflected in the response to the public announcement about building literacy teams for a national campaign. The people in Bulawayo, central city in the south, insisted that they would not come for a training session in Harare. We would have to do two trainings: one for the north in Harare, one for the south in Bulawayo.

In some ways this made our work easier. We would not be dealing with the tensions of a mixed set of political opinions among the trainees. It meant we had to design two training sessions for two very different groups. We had only one representative of the southern group on the training design team. He was a strong man, a church leader, and he struggled courageously to have his voice heard. If dialogue education is a way to structure listening and learning, the making of this training design team was excellent practice. We had to listen to one another and share leadership. As an external consultant, I realized how little I knew and understood of Zimbabwe's history and culture. Leadership roles on the team went to those like Ms. Mudondo who represented the literacy coordinators whom these trainers would be teaching. We had to listen to those representing the national factions, too, like our friend from Bulawayo.

The teams had to reflect the structure of the rural and urban society they were addressing. We, on the design team, were not to decide who would be accepted as literacy coordinators. We knew, however, that we had to give explicit attention in the training to the issue of respect for the adult learners to whom these young people would be teaching literacy skills. The pressure of the political moment precluded the kind of needs assessment that would have been most appropriate for this design team.

The report of the Nicaraguan Literacy Crusade indicates how they did needs assessment there before their literacy campaign: "The core team spent the first month studying—reading about the experiences of other countries, discussing the small church-sponsored literacy projects that had been attempted in Nicaragua, talking with experts, writing position papers, and outlining a possible primer. At the end of September, the core team of seven visited Cuba for a week" (Cardenal and Miller, 1981, p. 10).

A lesson from all this is the need for a team to form its own consensus over time and become a unit with an integrated focus. When this does not happen, when time is not given to such preparation, the team and the project pay for it throughout the entire program.

A Pedagogy of Shared Responsibility

The slogan used by the Nicaraguan Literacy Crusade in their orientation program to train the immense teacher corps of high school and college students in the Nicaraguan program was, "A Pedagogy of Shared Responsibility." The Zimbabwe team used the Nicaraguan experience as a framework for designing the training of literacy coordinators. In Nicaragua, the teacher's manual provided step-by-step instruction on the use of the literacy methodology and also contained detailed back-up readings for each of the twenty-three themes. It gave the young literacy teachers, called *brigadistas,* the necessary social, political, and economic information to generate a knowledgeable discussion and dialogue. Since the crusade was considered a reciprocal learning process, the handbook also outlined a systematic set of study activities for the volunteers. The basis of their learning was their own living and teaching experience. As such, they were responsible for conducting a careful research study of their communities and keeping a field diary of their activities (Cardenal and Miller, 1981, p. 19).

There were significant differences between the Zimbabwean and Nicaraguan campaigns. Zimbabwe's literacy coordinators would be paid staff of the Ministry of Education. The Nicaraguan campaign used youthful volunteers from the schools.

The design I proposed for the training of literacy coordinators incorporated some of the reciprocity issues named by the Nicaraguan crusade. The coordinators would be learners as well as teachers. If we were to do this training well, it would not only be Zimbabwe's preliterate men and women who would learn, but the coordinators as well.

The Program and the Process

We made work teams the basis of the entire experience. These young people had very recently been on military teams, driving a tank together or flying a fighter plane. They had seven years' experience of military teamwork. How was this new team experience to be similar for them? How would it be different? My concern in the design was for demonstrating the kind of respect and listening that we all knew was essential if the young people whom team members were to train were to reach the hearts of their elders in the villages whom they would be teaching how to read and write. I could bring technical expertise, and I did. I could bring planning, design, and evaluation skills, and I did. But I knew all too well that these skills were not the heart of the matter. The heart of the matter lay in the meaning and potential of the dialogue that would have to occur among team members and between literacy coordinators and the adult student. Their first job was to learn to listen to one another in their own team and show respect to one another in new and appropriate ways. On the first day of training, we invited each team to decide together on a name for their learning team related to the recent war of liberation. Many chose names of their friends who had died in the struggle for independence. They were deeply moved as they introduced themselves and their teams by these honored names.

Using a strong element in African culture, we invited teams to create or share songs they could use in teaching. Early on, in the first training, a group of six men and women began to sing the marching song they had sung as guerrilla soldiers: "The Soldier's Song." It was a beautiful moment, as the whole group took it up quite spontaneously. At that moment of the training workshop, the difficulties they had experienced getting selected for this job, the confusion and ambiguity about their role, all fell aside and they found themselves restored to the unity of purpose of a team that had won a war of independence. These two team tasks, naming their learning teams and selecting a song, had achieved what was needed to get us started with the training in how to teach and how to use the Zimbabwean literacy materials. They had worked as a team, made decisions with some consensus, observed leadership emerge among themselves. There were no lieutenants and captains now, no stripes or rank. Team leadership would emerge by action.

When setting learning tasks for teams by the use of open questions, the teacher is admitting that she does not know "the" answer to the question. The facilitator has no control over what the team will say or how it will respond. We found that the leadership of one team's sharing "The Soldiers' Song" evoked a great deal of energy in the other teams to do as well or better. This is the element of *com + petition* (asking together) that such teamwork offers. These young men and women were challenging one another, asking how far they could go together. The Nicaraguan training used a Central American genre called the *couplet*, a popular Latin literary expression. In Zimbabwe, we used the *methali* or proverb to summarize or question what we were learning. Each team selected a familiar proverb, or made one up, at the end of each day to synthesize all that they had learned about teaching literacy that day. "One hand does not wash itself!" "On the third day the guest receives a hoe!" Such proverbs caught the wisdom of the language and the people.

It was not hard to find preliterate adults for practice teaching classes in Harare, where we did the first training course. We happened to be at the University of Zimbabwe and were able to enroll a small group of workers who cleaned and kept the grounds as learners in the first round of the program. The teams decided who would teach and how they would arrange the situation so that they could both observe their colleague and respect the learner. Each team selected a set of evaluation indicators that was then reviewed by the entire group. They held their friend's feet to the fire with those indicators. We did some work beforehand on how to give and get feedback so that there would be no defensiveness and no attacks

(Vella, 1995, pp. 50–51). The practice teaching sessions were an excellent chance to test the written materials, as well. As these were still in draft form, the young people knew that their recommendations would be given serious attention. We did not have the luxury of a video camera at these practice teaching sessions. If we had, the videos could have been reviewed by the entire team, and the learning would have been shared by all. When we use video as we do today for practice teaching, the learning is immediate, affective, and effective, and the data are objective.

Evaluation

Immediate evaluation of learning—measuring how well they knew they knew—told us that all the young people in both sites, north and south, could demonstrate the skills they needed to design and teach literacy. Their practice teaching sessions were personally rewarding to themselves and to the adult students. They felt and demonstrated a bond to their team members.

The teamwork aspects of this training program were sound. There is no way these men and women could have learned what they learned in six days without having done so in those working teams. Team tasks were sometimes completed without any intervention from trainers. Ms. Mudondo worked as a team member, and I was out of the loop because teams often worked in their own language. Their learning in their teams was both autonomous and independent. Such autonomy and independence is the deeper purpose of a literacy campaign. The people of Zimbabwe did not simply need to learn to read and write; they needed to learn to work together as members of village and community teams to create their new nation.

Impact evaluation, the effect of this training session on their future work as team members of the ministry managing the literacy campaign, was less encouraging. We had designed a careful sequence of tasks in the six-day training workshop, but there was not a careful sequence of follow-up work with the teams of literacy trainers after they started their work of training coordinators. The team structure, used so well in the training sessions, was not used for follow-up and support of the literacy staff in their widespread teaching posts around the country. Ms. Mudondo was not in a position of power at the ministry to get systems for follow-up and support of the teams of literacy teachers in the field. If they had maintained the team structure, even with teams of two, and nurtured those roles and relationships, they might have created a long-lasting program.

Quantum theory teaches that the whole is greater than the sum of its parts. As a practice, teams are useful. As a principle, team is essential. The Ministry of Education had yet to learn this. The political fragmentation of the time affected the whole effort.

Design Challenges

- The dialogue approach naturally invites people to work in teams. What happens in the teams is not vicarious: it is real life! There is no "getting back to reality" but rather a getting *down* to reality in doing a learning task as a team. This puts the burden on us to compose teams wisely and well. Teams may be composed by the adult learners themselves; they may be composed by the teacher's putting similar or different people together; they may be composed by chance. In any case, the composition is intentional. And it is your responsibility. What have you learned from the Zimbabwe story about composing teams in your next training event?

- A learning task done by a team involves peer pressure and many overt and hidden dynamics within the group. Quantum theory shows us the importance of context. As you saw in this example from Zimbabwe, the political fragmentation of north and south affected the literacy campaign. The team is a group of adults, and the responsibility to learn is theirs. Your responsibility is to compose teams and prepare a well-formed educational design. You cannot learn for others. The team, or small group, is there to help members learn. Your detachment is of value to yourself and to the adult learners. How can you show that you trust the team? Consider a time when you, as teacher, wanted to interfere in a team or small-group activity. What was the advantage to you—and to them—of resisting that temptation by "sitting still, keeping quiet, and paying attention"?

14

Engagement
Learning Actively

Throughout this book you have seen the power of engagement
to enhance learning through learning tasks; praxis; teamwork;
safe cognitive, affective, and action challenges; and needs assessment. In Chapter One you read a summary statement of the efficacy
of engagement.

This is a story of the power of engagement as a principle of adult
learning—a principle that enables learners not only to take part
in learning but also to practice learning as subjects of their own
lives. In this case study we see the learners take an active role not
only in learning but also in the design and structure of their own
future as an organization.

The Situation

Hospice as a health care movement has been growing like the
proverbial Topsy. There is an immense need for the loving care of
hospice nurses, social workers, chaplains, volunteers, and aides who
come to the homes of the sick to serve not only the patient but also
the families of those who have been diagnosed with limited life expectancy. The growing threat of AIDS has made the growth of hospice care even more critical.

In eastern North Carolina, an inter-county hospice found itself growing larger and larger as more and more families applied for

service. The communities were getting more involved, and so the volunteer cadre was increasing. The funding base was constantly strained and the need for more resources—personnel, finances, improved systems—was obvious. The executive director, a caring nurse and an astute administrator, realized it was time to do some strategic planning. As she said, very wisely, "We must all learn to think strategically. This growth will continue!"

She was determined to make this planning process inclusive by engaging as many staff and board and community members as possible. She invited us at the Jubilee Education Center to design and lead the program. How could we use the principles and practices of dialogue education to engage the entire hospice community in planning for their future? Here quantum thinking would help. We recognized that the whole organization was in need. That whole was much more than the sum of its parts. How could we use the principle of engagement in the early planning steps of a strategic planning session to work with the whole organization?

The Learners

This hospice community was a model of diversity: on staff were nurses, physicians, administrators, physicians' aides, accountants, aides, chaplains, social workers, and volunteers. Some had been with this hospice since its beginning two decades ago; others were newcomers. Some had graduate degrees; others had completed high school. We made it clear from the beginning of our planning that all voices were welcome. The policy and program priorities that might evolve through this strategic plan were decisions of the hospice's management team, which comprises department directors from nursing, volunteer services, and administration. Once these priorities were set by that team, the board of directors had to approve them in light of the available budget.

Officially, the executive director had the deliberative voice— that is, she made the decisions. She wisely shared this voice with the management team. All others, throughout the planning session, had a consultative voice—that is, they made suggestions. Once this distinction was made clear, the process could work smoothly. All would be engaged; some would make the final decisions. If this distinction is not made in organizations, participants who are engaged in naming priority issues and program innovations may wrongly expect all their suggestions to become policy. The distinction clarifies each person's role and invites creative thinking. It enables engagement and enhances learning.

The Program and the Process

All the principles and practices of dialogue education worked here to bring many people together in a planning process that actually led at the end to a feasible three-year plan for the hospice. The exciting prime principle in this case was the engagement of all hospice staff.

We at Jubilee first studied all the documents we could lay our hands on dealing with the history of this hospice. We studied the demographics and were shocked at the size of the growth. We spoke with a sample of staff and board members to get a sense of the mood and status of the program as well as the organizational development. Their engagement with us in this data gathering gave us a sense of the diversity of perspectives at work. Through the community survey, we were able to hear from a wide sample of the clients as well. We were actually honoring the quantum concept of participation, aware that each person created the hospice they perceived.

A community survey form was given to each staff person, who was then asked to select and survey one person in the community they served whose opinion they valued. There were three questions on the survey:

1. What has been your personal experience of hospice?
2. What one thing in hospice do you value most?
3. What one thing would you like hospice to do that we are not doing?

We had a 70 percent return of these surveys and presented all the raw data to the staff to use during the one-day workshop. This was the means of engaging the wider community in this strategic planning process and demonstrating to the staff that they were the vital link between the hospice and that community. Selecting the person they surveyed was practice in autonomy, demonstrating that they were indeed subjects of this process. The voice of the community was heard also through the board members and the cadre of volunteers. What was at work were three quantum concepts: relatedness, energy, and a holistic perception. The whole community and staff of hospice saw how they were personally related, one to the other, and how the work of hospice related directly to the community. The energy of the community was raised by inviting them to offer their ideas on *their* hospice; energy of the staff was raised by the comprehensive inclusion. Finally, a holistic perception was at work as everyone saw their part essential to the whole well-being of the organization.

We used the basic outline for strategic planning from John Bryson's *Strategic Planning for Public and Nonprofit Organizations* (1988) and the seven steps of design to set out a draft program to engage all three groups of participants: staff, board, and management team. Bryson gives a sequence of concepts: stakeholders, mission, SWOT (strengths, weaknesses, opportunities, threats), strategic issues, strategies, action plan. We used the seven steps of design—*who, why, when, what for, what, where, how*—to design appropriate tasks that would engage all participants in responding to these strategic planning steps.

In terms of the time frame—the *when* in the seven steps—we arranged to work with three sets of participants (the *who*). First we worked with all the staff. All seventy-six staff members, including the management team, came freely to the one-day workshop. Three staff members interrupted their vacations to attend. They wanted their consultative voices to be heard in the design of the strategic plan for hospice. We had a second one-day workshop with the board of directors and management team, and finally we had a day-long workshop with the management team, which tied it all together and prepared a plan for the board to review.

Here is one learning task from the program. It was used to define strengths, weaknesses, opportunities, threats (a SWOT analysis):

- *What* (content): strengths, weaknesses; opportunities, threats

- *What for* (achievement based objective): Participants will have prepared a SWOT analysis including internal strengths and weaknesses, external opportunities and threats.

- *How*

    Task A. A SWOT analysis names internal strengths and weaknesses, external opportunities and threats. At your tables of four, identify all the strengths of this hospice and write them on the chart on your table. We'll hear a sample and record them all. No perception will be excluded.

    Task B. Identify all the weaknesses you perceive in this hospice at present. We'll hear a sample and record them all.

    Task C. Name the opportunities you see facing this hospice. We'll hear a sample and record them all.

    Task D. Name the threats you see facing this hospice. We'll hear a sample and record them all.

Each table had a chart on which to record participants' work. These charts were copied into the report, which was used by the participants in the next session. By inviting and honoring their perceptions, we were actually taking a holistic view of the organization from a quantum perspective.

The immediate relation of content, objective, and task drew all groups into intense engagement, especially because the time frame for doing this particular learning task was quite short. We have discovered that the shorter the time frame for a task, the higher the energy. Notice that the SWOT analysis was entirely inductive; that is, the factors learned were named by the participants from their firsthand experience of the hospice.

The aims of the daylong strategic planning workshop were set out as achievement based objectives: *By the end of this day, we all will have*

- Named symbols of our work in hospice

- Identified stakeholders in hospice by using data from each hospice's community survey

- Edited the new mission statement

- Prepared a SWOT analysis (internal strengths and weaknesses; external opportunities and threats)

- Identified strategic issues in this hospice today and selected one from each table cluster

- Named one practical alternative that would address this issue

- Identified the barriers to this practical alternative

- Prepared a proposal for implementation

These objectives were achieved in a six-hour period by seventy-six staff and four board members by having them do small-group tasks at tables of four. This arrangement ensured comprehensive engagement. Even the most reticent staff person could raise her voice in such a setting. As we gathered data from all the tables, we noticed a growing consensus of attitude and opinion. We also heard dissenting voices that were honored. The report of this six-hour meeting, which recorded the tasks that completed the nine objectives, was thirty-six pages long. This was the database offered to the board before they began their similar workshop.

The comprehensive engagement of all staff members was informed by the response of community members to the survey. This staff report in turn informed the work of the board of directors, who enhanced the database for the strategic plan through their suggestions. They added their perceptions to those of the staff and proceeded to name priority issues for action. Finally, the management team faced this mass of data and distilled it into a specific set of action plans, which they later presented to the full meeting of the board of directors. That is indeed engagement.

What looked like chaos in the wide range of responses from community and staff was soon seen to have an intrinsic order. Here is quantum thinking! Zohar quotes Dee Hock of VISA (Zohar, 1997, p. 133) who named such a process "chaordic."

Evaluation

Immediate evaluation of the learning and progress toward a viable strategic plan indicated that all participants were surprised at how well they had achieved the nine achievement based objectives. The accountable design of the program, based on all the principles and practices of dialogue education, ensured that outcome. People were in small groups, mixed as to their role in hospice, and worked as teams to achieve the objectives. Team reports were enhanced by the individual voices that were raised to say: "My team said this, but I feel differently." This was an indication of the safety they felt in the room.

Here the educational objectives were also production objectives because they were generating data for future use in a strategic plan. We, as facilitators, shifted the tasks to fit the time so that the six hours available for the workshop were fruitful. There was incredible energy in the room. Since all participants were there of their own volition—as subjects of this operation—they were vigorous in their effort and daringly honest. Their engagement was at once the means to the end of producing the strategic plan and also a means to enhance their perception of themselves as one hospice team. The operative question for short-term evaluation of a dialogue education function like this is, *How do they know they know?* In this case, all who were engaged in this process celebrated their engagement by the fact that many of their suggestions were visible in the agency's new plan and new priorities. How do they know they know strategic thinking and planning? They just did it.

The chaplain and president of the board of directors both made this comment to the director about the workshop process: "These folks from Jubilee are tough!" They meant we had a design that would not let participants stray from the purpose. The design, and our relentless implementation of it, demanded intense engagement.

What about the long-term indicators of transfer (the use of skills learned) and impact (changes in organization as a result of the learning)? Not only is a strategic plan in place for this hospice team and community but action is also under way on a number of fronts. They have a Gantt chart (calendar) that is used daily to measure their progress, as well as a common language that all can use to identify and change priorities. The impact of a planning process like this in a large community agency is manifold. The agency not only has an effective plan in place but it also has a more conscious team at work in the hospice office, the community, and the homes of patients. A useful question for impact evaluation of community education like this strategic planning session is, *So what?* After some years, there are strong indicators that the focus of this hospice is clear and priorities are in place to handle future growth.

Design Challenges

- What are some of the indicators you now use in your educational programs to show that adult learners are fully engaged?

- What is the advantage to you as teacher when adult learners are engaged, working in small groups or teams, completing learning tasks, and raising their voices with suggestions or even protests about your program?

- What do you see as the advantage to the agency's management team of having so many people engaged in the preparation of a strategic plan?

- How are the following six quantum concepts related to the principle of engagement for you?

  Relatedness: All that we do in design and teaching is related.

  Holistic perspective: The whole is far more than the sum of its parts. Learners learn more than we teach!

  Duality: Embrace the opposites, use "both/and" thinking (light is a particle and a wave). Open questions invite both/and thinking and dialogue.

  Uncertainty: Every theory is constantly being constructed by application to new contexts. We do not control another's learning.

  Participation: The observer is part of what she observes. Each person's perception of any given reality is different, dependent on their context and culture. We evoke the world we perceive.

  Energy: Product is dependent on process. Learning demands energy.

15

Accountability
Knowing How They Know They Know

In Chapter One you read a short summary of the principle of accountability. By accountability we mean that the teacher is responsible to teach what he has promised learners will learn. And the learners are responsible to do the work of learning. Accountability is a mutual principle.

Considering adult educators accountable to their learners is a startling principle, especially when those educators are physicians. At the world-famous International Center for Diarrheal Disease Control (ICDDC) in Dacca, Bangladesh, a small group of physicians invited me to teach them the principles and practices of dialogue education during a single week of training. I have worked with teaching physicians at the University of North Carolina Medical School and with young interns at Duke Medical School, as well as with doctors in Save the Children programs and physicians from the Pontifical Catholic University in Chile. Few of these doctors had ever previously examined their teaching approach.

The Situation and the Setting

In the ICDDC the task of teaching patients how to prevent diarrheal disease was a vital part of the curative and preventative program. This was a referral hospital that received cases that could not be handled at the local level throughout Bangladesh. For these patients, who arrived close to death and then left the hospital with a new lease on life, this was the teachable moment. The family crisis around their coming to Dacca and staying at the hospital certainly got the attention of their local community. Indeed, they were often the patient celebrities of their villages.

What doctors knew as teaching methods—telling these recovering patients how to prevent a recurrence of this horrible situation for themselves or for other members of their family—was simply not working. The staff saw patients come in again and again. They saw other members of the same family arrive, drawn and dehydrated, as near death as any human being can be. The spoken message was simply not getting through.

Public health campaigns on the issue of diarrheal disease control have proliferated in Bangladesh. Although this training of a small number of doctors in dialogue education was not a major component of the national campaign, a few physicians from this prestigious hospital who began to consider alternative ways to teach these adults could make a new beginning. We all understood this. The doctors were practical men and women. They gave their time to this educational program because they knew their present paradigm was not working.

The Learners

Assura Lori is a middle-aged grandmother, a bustling, dynamic woman who raised a family of four sons. She is also a busy physician with her own medical practice, working in clinics and hospitals and continually doing research on the number one killer in Bangladesh: diarrhea. She holds a professor's chair at the University in Dacca and works tirelessly at ICDDC trying to prevent the epidemic disease. It was she who heard about the community education efforts of Save the Children and contacted a Washington-based funding source to explore a training program for doctors at this hospital. The funds came through and I headed to Dacca with virtually no information about the physicians with whom I would be working. I knew only that they would be doctors on the staff of ICDDC and, therefore, men and women of long experience. They would be middle-aged or older. My gray hair and long years of experience in Africa, Asia, and Latin America would at least get their attention. I needed to know a great deal more about the group, about how they taught, the central issues of the hospital, and their personal achievements. This learning needs and resources assessment was going to be tough but very necessary.

Even for my travel-worn eyes, Dacca was a shock. Not since Calcutta had I seen so many people in one place at one time and such evident, gnawing poverty and hunger. I met Lori at her office in the hospital that first day, and she wisely gave me some things to read and sent me off to sleep for the day. "Otherwise," she smiled, "we shall be dealing with your jet lag for the whole time!" I thought: sleep can deal with physical jet lag; nothing can deal with the cultural jet lag experienced by a well-fed American arriving in Dacca, Bangladesh, visiting the Hospital for the Control of Diarrheal Disease. I felt once again the overwhelming humility I had felt in Mali, Ethiopia, Tanzania, Kenya, El Salvador. I had come to teach and knew I would stay to learn. While such humility in the face of the complexities of an unfamiliar culture may be healthy, it is not a very pleasant feeling, for it comes mixed generously with rank fear: What in the world am I doing here? How dare I teach these people?

Sleep did help. The gnawing fear never went away, however, and I believe it is well that I felt it. Carl Jung (1969, p. 4) teaches: "Whoever reflects upon himself meets the frontiers of the unconscious, which holds all he needs to know." I would soon find that my honesty in dealing with this fear would be demanded again and again as I worked to teach these physicians the principles and practices of dialogue education.

I spent two days at the hospital at the bedside of frail and withered men, women, and children suffering from diarrheal disease, interviewing the doctors who would take the course, talking to nurses and aides about their work. These nurses and aides, I discovered, were the true patient educators, apparently more effective than all the doctors. For the training course, however, we had to begin at the top. This was a political decision in which I played no part. The hope was that these doctors would teach the nurses and aides what they had learned. I knew this would not happen in any formal way. Busy physicians do not have that kind of time. I realized there and then how vital it is to be in a position to select the participants in such a course if there were to be optimal replication of skills and knowledge. However, one does what one can at the time. Lori invited me to her clinic in the city where she saw patients before sending them to ICDDC. I saw families dealing with this overwhelming and endemic reality with quiet submission. These were the adult learners whom the doctors faced every day. How would the principles of adult learning help the physicians to teach these folks what they needed to know?

The doctors did not know that Bangladesh has been a wellspring of research on dialogue education. The country lends itself, with its vast numbers of rural and urban illiterate needing to know so much to cope in a new industrial society, to such an approach. Indeed, dialogue education centers throughout the country have produced excellent materials on literacy, agriculture, health, and management of small industries. I realized that these centers could be valuable resources for follow-up on the skills, knowledge, and attitudes learned this week by the small cadre of doctors. In my preparation for the week, I visited one of the education centers near Dacca. Political reasons kept these centers from serving the local medical profession but they were very supportive of my effort, minuscule as it was in the face of their national dilemmas. They offered me all the materials they had developed on the issue of health and graciously offered to serve as a referral for the physicians after the course.

Lori and I spent three days hammering out a program that would be relevant and immediate for these physicians. I realized at once that the participant physicians would not be present for all the sessions, since the course would take place at the hospital and all of them would be on call for emergencies with their patients. Regular hospital meetings had to be attended throughout the week, as well. We found ourselves planning a course to take place in the interstices of their days.

This phenomenon is one I have met in virtually all of the forty countries where I have worked as an educator. The fact is that education is rarely a priority. There is nothing we can do about this attitude directly. We must simply face it and name it. In Swahili there is a wise proverb: *Ubora hauhitaji sifa* ("Excellence needs no praise"). Our task as educators is to make the learning so accountable, the engagement so meaningful, immediacy so useful, that this unhealthy attitude will change in time. As long as education continues to "resist dialogue" (Freire, 1972, p. 71) and is not accountable, engaging, or immediate, as long as it continues to be what Donald Oliver (1989) calls "miseducation," such a lack of respect for the process will continue.

The Program and the Process

Lori and I started to design, with the time available to us, in the place available to us. My fear and trepidation rose as we worked out the seven steps of design for the course.

- *Who* (learners). The learners would be the twelve physicians from the ICDDC, eight men and four women, all with long experience in medicine. They each volunteered to take this course.
- *Why.* Situation: ICDDC is a teaching hospital not only for the university medical school but also for the patients and their families. The formal education methods these doctors know from their own experience in medical school and professional training do not work with unlettered (often preliterate) Bangladeshi citizens who come to this hospital. The doctors, as I watched them with their patients and the other health professionals, were comfortable

talking about the situation as an abstract problem. They stayed in their heads, even during an educational session with desperately sick patients and their families. These doctors, indeed, all the staff of ICDDC, needed a process of dialogue education that would be accountable to patients and their families alike, so that they would know they knew when they left the hospital.

Outcomes: The twelve doctors will be able to identify principles and practices of dialogue education and use these to design courses for nurses and aides as well as for direct patient and family education.

• *When* (timeframe). I insisted we should organize the course so that all participants attended all learning sessions. In light of the inevitable emergency calls and regular hospital meetings, that gave us the possibility of four hours a day. This decision was made to avoid having people coming in and out of the course. It emerged from my experience that when one person enters or leaves a group, it becomes a new group. The intensity of training in dialogue education, the fact that learning tasks are done in small groups, the fact that bonding takes place among learners—all justified this decision to work in a shorter time frame with all twelve participants. It was also an opportunity to model with the physicians the principles of respect and inclusion that we were teaching them to use when training other health care personnel in this approach. Four hours for six days gave us the modest total of twenty-four hours with the group. It was a challenge to select the most useful content and learning tasks for this time frame.

• *Where* (site). There was no way these physicians could leave the hospital for a week. Their responsibilities kept them close to patients and colleagues. So the course had to take place at the hospital in a dark, windowless meeting room with a rusty old air conditioner filling the space with a steady noise and cold blasts of recycled air. This meeting room had one large old table that filled the central space. It was designed for a hierarchy: the teacher at the head of the table and doctors ranked by status around it. This was the room in which staff development sessions took place as well, so their memories of other events in the room would be competing with our approach. Our challenge was to structure small group sessions around that table in ways that could work for the doctors.

• *What.* The rich content of the course would include the skills, knowledge, and attitudes they would learn: the principles and practices of dialogue education; the affective, cognitive, and psychomotor aspects of learning; theories of communication; the design and use of open questions; themes of learners; communication modes (direct, indirect) and theories of communication; the difference between monologue and dialogue; the learner as subject (never object); design of learning tasks; design of learning materials using dialogue; evaluation indicators (immediate and long-term) of learning, transfer, and impact.

• *What for.* Lori and all the physicians had been given copies of my book *Learning to Teach* (1989) and were frankly not impressed by the simplicity of the approach. Lori and I struggled to design immediate, engaging objectives that would challenge this sophisticated group of professional men and women. She was admittedly frightened by the simplicity of the tasks. These people, of course, were used to dealing with complex quantitative data and reading journal articles replete with specialized language. Although I was tempted to couch the principles and practices of dialogue education in such epistemological jargon that they might be duly impressed, I overcame the temptation and held my ground. Dialogue education involves a complex and subtle technical form. There is no need to codify that complexity and subtlety in esoteric language or jargon. I told her that I was offering them an alternative approach to adult learning designed for the real world. If they wanted to explore it, we would do so in simple terms and clear learning tasks. The principles and practices of dialogue education are expressed in the language of dialogue. If they wanted esoteric language and studied complexity, they had the wrong teacher.

At this point, I recognized I could not compromise without losing the whole purpose of the project. I was there with what I knew of dialogue education. It might or might not work in ICDDC, but we had to try it—not some rarefied version of it designed to fit into what was clearly an unhealthy mold. This moment felt not unlike the moment in Ethiopia when Fatuma and her rifle saved my day. Where was Fatuma when I needed her in Bangladesh? Lori took a deep breath and admitted: "You are right. If what you offer does not help us teach these people what they need to know to survive, we can decide that later. Right now, this week, you must teach us as you know best." I assured her that her decision would at least give us a chance to model dialogue education with the doctors.

This is one of the most compelling aspects of dialogue education. You must use the principles and practices to teach the principles and practices, or else you do not teach them accountably. It is as simple as that. To use what Paulo Freire named "the banking approach," to talk about dialogue education as if it were an abstraction, is not only *not* to teach it but is actually teaching the opposite. Taking a holistic approach to the course is good quantum thinking.

So we accepted some basic achievement based objectives for the doctors: *By the end of these six days (twenty-four hours), we all will have*

1. Identified the educational issues of ICDDC

2. Shared stories of successful learning events with preliterate learners

3. Reviewed adult learning theories of Knowles, Lewin, Vella

4. Designed open questions and practiced using them

5. Completed a thematic analysis of a sample of patients, discovering their themes, or issues that move them

6. Distinguished affective, cognitive, and psychomotor aspects of learning (feelings, ideas, actions)

7. Identified familiar communication modes of Bangladeshi families

8. Reviewed and adapted useful theories of communication

9. Examined cultural possibilities for communication in song, drama, dance, film, video, radio

10. Examined the difference between monologue and dialogue

11. Designed materials for preliterate and literate patients and families using the seven steps of design

12. Designed a set of learning tasks using these materials

13. Evaluated this course daily and made course corrections for greater immediacy and engagement and ultimate accountability

• *How.* The physicians would learn dialogue education by doing it. I wanted to be sure we gave these twelve doctors a real taste of this new approach, so the learning tasks were somewhat more radical than usual. Having seen them in action with their patients and staff (even though I did not understand the language), I knew we had to give them a chance to get out of their heads and into their hands and hearts. I insisted also on videotaping the program from beginning to end. This would give us a chance at replication, a document for the funding group, and a useful monitor to show the funding group that the doctors had indeed been present for all twenty-four hours. We used the video during the course for feedback and evaluation, as well. The funding organization that had sent me to Bangladesh agreed to provide resources for hiring a professional video technician and for equipment and processing. I would urge all educators to ensure this useful tool is in the budget for every educational program.

Evaluation

Daily formative evaluations offered us more and more input on the overall design of the course so we could make it more and more immediate for the physicians. The open questions of the evaluation process—What was most useful for you today? What shall we change tomorrow?—gave them emotional freedom to object to tasks that seemed culturally inappropriate and demand tasks more immediate to their needs. Because of the need for immediacy in this process, I accepted most of their suggestions. By now, they had the deliberative voice in the course. They themselves asked for more hours each day. This itself was an indicator of learning.

For long-term evaluation we put them in touch with the director of the Bangladesh Research and Action Center (BRAC), where they could get materials and further instruction in dialogue education. There were no systems in place, however, to reward such efforts, nor was there ongoing funding. Today I am convinced that single events such as this course in Bangladesh are somewhat futile. They might make a difference in the approach of one or more doctors. However, without organized follow-up and systems for rewarding new learning and revised efforts, the burden on the individual is too great to be sustained. I often say there are three things that make accountable learning happen: time, time, and time. Without reinforcement, without a sequence of continued learning activities and a research agenda on the epistemology, without the stimulation of appropriate rewards and motivation, professionals will go back to teaching the way they were taught. The key quantum concept of seeing a program as a whole is operative here.

The enthusiasm of these twelve doctors and their animated engagement during the short course were perhaps a function of my involvement with them. What did they need to sustain that quality of learning at the hospital? We created in those six days what Oliver and Gershman (1989) call an occasion of being and knowing. However, once again, we did not create a system for sustaining the learning.

What happened for the twelve doctors in Bangladesh? They got out of their heads, freed somewhat from the abstractions of diarrhea as a disease and a research agenda. They moved into their hearts and hands as they practiced new ways of approaching patients and their families. The question all adult educators face is this: How can we make these "occasions of being and knowing" occur systemically?

How can we professionals, such as doctors, lawyers, social workers, and teachers, create self-regulating programs with rewards and systems for continuation so that the work we do is accountable?

Design Challenges

- What would you have done differently if you had arrived in Dacca, as I did, with the mandate to teach a group of physicians the elements of dialogue education in one week?

- What do you now understand about accountability? How will you use this principle in your work?

- How can you change a course you are now teaching to make it more immediately useful for the learners? How can you win their deeper engagement? And how can you prove to yourself and to your adult learners that your teaching is accountable?

- Which quantum concepts did you see visibly at work at the International Center for Diarrheal Disease Control during the short workshop?

Part III

Becoming an Effective
Teacher of Adults

16

Reviewing the Twelve Principles and Quantum Thinking

Having persevered this far through the stories and having done some of the design challenges, you are now familiar enough with the selected principles and practices of adult learning to use them in your designs. You probably recognize that you are already using many of them in your teaching. As one group of adult educators in Chile told me: "We have been doing this for years. We just didn't know what to call it!" Knowing what to call the principles can be a guide to using them intentionally in our adult learning designs.

While we honor the teaching style (that is, the personality) of each teacher, we also honor the transcendence of these principles. Adult educators will use the principles in ways that reflect their own teaching styles, but the principles remain the same. The characteristics of a particular group of learners are defined as we use the seven steps of design and begin with the *who*. All our decisions about tasks and materials, sequence and reinforcement, evaluation and application, are informed by our reflection on the learners' profile. Tasks appropriate for a group of twenty-five-year-old National Service recruits will not be effective with a group of senior citizens. Respect for the *who* informs our designs in dialogue education. We remember the quantum concept of participation: Each person's perception of any given reality is different. It is dependent on their context and culture. We evoke the world we perceive.

The Principles in Action

We have focused on these twelve principles and practices: needs assessment; safety; sound relationships; sequence and reinforcement; praxis (action with reflection); respect for learners as subjects of their learning; cognitive, affective, and psychomotor aspects of learning (ideas, feelings, actions); immediacy; clear roles; teamwork in small groups; engagement; and accountability. We have shown how the seven steps of design focus our preparation of a learning design. Now we will see these principles once again in action.

Learning Needs and Resources Assessment

In your programs, a needs assessment can be done in a variety of ways. If you are teaching young entrepreneurs how to start a business, you could try a telephone survey of a sample of those registered for your course. In that survey you might ask: What are your greatest fears? What are your hopes for your small business? What are the three areas you feel you need to learn about? If you use a written survey, you can list all the potential content of your course and invite course participants to indicate which three items seem most important to them.

If you are teaching young people in college a life skill such as responsible parenting, this principle guides you in choosing how you will discover what they already know about this intimate subject and what they think they need to know for their own safety and personal development. Using a case study of a young couple making tough decisions about intimacy and marriage can enable the group of young learners to manifest and assess their own learning needs. As they analyze and suggest changes in a complex case, they show where their own knowledge is lacking and where they need to develop clearer attitudes about sensitive issues. This case study can be a part of the learning design, or it can be used prior to the session. Learning needs and resources assessment is a continuous process: we discover learners' needs, we meet them, and in doing so through engaging tasks we discover further needs.

Suppose you are teaching organic gardening to an avid group of men and women who want to raise vegetables for their own families. How do you know what they need to know? Ask them! Study their experience and their educational profile. Observe them in the garden. How about going to the homes of a small sample of the group to see how they have set up their family vegetable gardens? When you come to mine, you would immediately discover a great deal that I obviously need to know. Designing innovative ways to do the three needs assessment tasks—ask, study, observe—is your constant challenge as an educator using dialogue education. The Appendix offers another set of suggestions for doing needs assessment.

Notice how needs assessment connects to immediacy for the learners, their consequent engagement in the learning tasks, and your accountability as an educator. This is quantum thinking: all these elements are related. When you honor one, you honor them all.

Safety

Establishing an environment of safety in the process and the setting of the learning, for learners and teacher, is both essential and challenging. Let's look at a National Service program, where young adults come to learn how to offer technical services to a community and work together as a team. How can we ensure they will feel safe enough in this venture to stay with it, do the job well, and be creative and critical in their response to the program? Other principles and practices come into play here: affirming, listening, echoing learners' words and feelings, having a sequence of learning tasks that is feasible and developmental, respecting learners as subjects of their lives and learning, establishing clear roles, and fostering accountability of leaders to the learners and to the program. Safety can be felt in a learning situation. These are some of the signs: laughter, a certain ease and camaraderie, a flow of questions from the learners, the teacher's invitation for comments on the process.

In a graduate course at the University of North Carolina School of Public Health, for example, the graduate students feel the safety I am trying to establish when they are invited to list their expectations of the course in light of the set objectives. I always tell them I will try to model the principles and practices of dialogue education I am teaching, and I invite their comments on that effort. By the fourth week of every semester, and usually only in the fourth week, a graduate student will question my decision to do something or will ask why I said what I said. It takes time for roles to change and for safety to work its magic toward honest dialogue.

Imagine the possibilities for such honest dialogue in an orientation program for new employees or a training program for police officers, firefighters, or nursing assistants. Again, the establishment of an environment of safety for oneself and the learners is part and parcel of preparing an effective learning design. Safety is deeply related to the quantum concept of energy. When adult learners feel safe, they bring more energy to their learning tasks; they take greater risks; they evoke a wider world for themselves.

Sound Relationships

A relationship of mutual respect between teacher and learner is often cited as the most important motivator of adult learners. There are many ways a teacher can develop this relationship.

In a course on English as a Second Language, the instructor invites learners to call him Mr. Jones and says he will call them by whatever name they wish. As each person says his or her name, the instructor writes it on the board in large letters (even though he has a registration list). He then greets the learner in English, using the name the learner has suggested. "Good evening, Miss Lao." A relationship of mutual respect is beginning.

In a community college woodworking class, the instructor gives the group his telephone number and invites them to call him whenever they're concerned about what they are doing in their home woodworking shops. This creates a sound relationship between learner and teacher, as the learner recognizes that the teacher is an accessible resource.

A physician working with a pregnant woman who is somewhat frightened by all the testing she faces can develop this sound relationship for learning by gently explaining the tests, inviting questions, and having a nurse accompany the woman with her spouse to the first test. Developing such a relationship takes time. Without that investment of time, however, the woman will perceive the physician as a technician, not a teacher. Perhaps HMOs that compel physicians to see twenty-five patients a day have forgotten that the root of *doctor* is the Latin verb *docere*, which means "to teach."

The quantum concept of participation is at work here. Each individual as observer evokes the world she observes. As the pregnant woman sees the physician as friend and ally, the doctor becomes just that.

Sequence and Reinforcement

How often must a skill, concept, or attitude be practiced in order for it to be known? In the intensive, weeklong Introduction to Dialogue Education courses, we find that adult learners need maximum amounts of reinforcement before they are able to design a session by using these principles and practices. Originally, we had set participants to the design task in teams so early that we almost always met resistance of one kind or another. Now, we work with them through a gentle set of well-sequenced tasks, reinforcing their skills in using the seven steps of design. They then design an achievement based objective, set an engaging learning task with clear resource materials, and evaluate their immediate learning. Learners do this once, review it, and then do it again before they set out to design a whole session.

We have learned that the design of learning tasks must reflect an appropriate sequence for the group and offer adequate reinforcement. Parents learning together how to care for their new infant need to have such learning tasks monitored by a nurse or assistant, sequenced to move from simple and safe to complex, and repeated until they indeed know they know. Their feeling of safety in the skill or knowledge is clearly manifest when they have had time to repeat a task or practice a skill.

New employees learning to work a complicated machine need to do the job with a mentor in small, well-sequenced tasks, then repeat it with guidance, then solo, again and again. Their smile of confidence and their agility with a complex series of maneuvers will be indicator enough that they know they know. Coaching is never mere telling. It is setting out a well-sequenced series of small tasks, repeating them often enough, getting learners back on course when they stray, and affirming them as they show their new skills. While such an effort seems to involve more time than the instructors can afford, we know it can save time and money in the long run. Learners will know their jobs better and will work with more confidence. The more competent the teaching (with sequence and reinforcement), the more capable the worker and the less time lost in correction and reteaching.

Such sequence and reinforcement do not take the challenge out of a tough learning situation. Quantum thinking assures us that nature is both chaotic and well-ordered ("chaordic") (Zohar, 1997, p. 133). We use sequence and reinforcement to enable learners to deal confidently with that chaos.

Praxis: Action with Reflection

As we reinforce a new skill, we invite a learner to practice it. Praxis—action with reflection—is more than practice. It means, as we have seen, that the learner does what she is learning and immediately reflects upon that doing. It is a collage of efforts: psychomotor, cognitive, and affective.

How does one "do" a new concept? If you were teaching new entrepreneurs how to keep their accounts, there are many concepts you would use: balance of expenses and income; debits and credits; deductible and nondeductible items. The learning tasks you set for them will be applications of these concepts. As learners complete each learning task, your next open question could be: How did you use the concept of balance in this task? When you invite such reflection, you change practice into praxis, action with reflection.

When adults begin to learn how to use a computer, praxis is vital. Simple tasks using concepts such as macros, hot keys, saving, formatting, and the skills related to each can be set in an appropriate sequence with adequate reinforcement. Then as each task is done, the concept or skill is made explicit through an open question: What macro was most useful to you in this task? Which hot key did you use? What is your common way of saving a file? Again, that is praxis: action with reflection. When we consciously use praxis in our design of learning tasks, the learners begin asking us questions—thinking critically not only about the content but also about the process. Praxis turns action into thought and back again. It is a wonderful combination of inductive and deductive learning: action into thought into new action. I see every learning task as praxis.

Respect for Learners as Subjects

No matter what you do, adult learners will learn what they need and want to know. This is at once a consoling and a challenging thought. A quantum concept reminds us that nature is self-regulating. In 1952, my professor of education theory, a tough old Irishman, said: "Ye needn't worry. They'll learn in spite of ye!" Our task is to show adult learners how to learn. We do that by showing them, in every way possible, our respect for them as subjects or decision makers of their learning. Consider this axiom: "Do not tell what you can ask. Do not ask if you know the answer; tell in dialogue." This invites the adult educator to honor the learner first as an adult with years of experience and informal as well as formal learning. Tapping this experience is one way to show respect. Inviting people to tell their stories, share their hopes and fears, and simply express their expectations of an educational event is a way to show this respect for them as subjects of their own lives, as well as of their own learning.

Literacy classes for the homeless are now part of the adult basic skills program of many states. In North Carolina, this program is managed through the community colleges. How can instructors design ways to demonstrate their respect for these unique learners who must practice being subjects of their own learning in this small area of their troubled lives? I have seen instructors invite homeless learners to tell the story of their best day, their worst night, their dream job. I have heard the poems of homeless literacy students who were invited by an instructor to tell their story in song or verse. Listening to learners' stories of their lives, their families, their hopes and dreams is a way of showing respect for them as subjects.

In a training course the mere invitation to learners to express their hopes and fears about the course and name their expectations is a simple way of showing respect and listening to them acting as subjects of their learning. We may not be able to meet all their expectations. That is not the issue. The issue is to listen respectfully. Then we can list the resources adults can use to meet the needs they have named.

Ideas, Feelings, and Actions

We have seen through these tales of learning and teaching the consistent use of three aspects of dialogue education: the cognitive (ideas), the affective (feelings), and the psychomotor (actions). Here is a principle we can put to immediate use as we design training or adult learning in any discipline. How is my teaching involving the learner in thinking, feeling, and doing? Where is the cognitive material in my content? Where is the affective? Where are the psychomotor aspects of the learning tasks I set?

A simple class in nutrition at a clinic can readily employ all these aspects if this principle is honored. The learners may read a story and see a picture of a hungry child. They may have been asked to bring to the class a small plate of food from their homes. The instructor adds other foods to the table, and the learners are invited to prepare, from all these foods, a simple meal for this child. I have a poignant memory of a day in a Caribbean country where a nurse, using her university training in nutrition education, stood in the shade of a mango tree that was dripping with ripe, mouth-watering mangoes. She was teaching a group of mothers how to feed their children. The nurse wanted to make the important point that fruit was important in the diet of children and infants. She had a series of large posters that she showed the women—pictures of mangoes and other fruit. Her lecture went on and on, the women dozed, their children squirmed in their arms. Perhaps, if she had known about the importance of this threefold set of learning factors, she might have had the mothers pick a mango, peel it, and feed it to their children. Her point could have been made as she invited reflection on that experience with the women. It could have been a moment of sweet praxis!

So much of our own education dealt with cognitive matter, without consideration of affective or psychomotor aspects, that it is a great temptation to tell people what they need or want to know. Setting achievement based objectives in our designs and shaping learning tasks to teach the content can help us recall and use this important principle of dialogue education. As Kurt Lewin (1951) puts it, learning is more effective when it is an active rather than a passive process.

Consider how you would use cognitive, affective, and psychomotor elements in designing to teach American history, teach a group of new citizens how to vote and why to vote, or teach the county workers at voting machines how to show senior citizens how easy it is to use them. The quantum concept of a holistic perception of our world comes into play here. We as educators cannot afford to leave out any one of these three—ideas, actions, feelings—as we design.

Immediacy

In Chapter Three, I showed an example of a training course for National Service workers in which immediacy was effective. You know that you have used this principle every time you see adult learners using what you have taught and celebrating the usefulness of it. In all kinds of adult learning, immediacy is a key motivator.

Coaching adults in their development of skills for any kind of trade involves this principle. You can show them how to use the first section of a skill, celebrate that, reflect on the process, and move on to the next part. The immediate success encourages the learners to begin to believe they can learn.

In a statistics course at a local university, a gifted teacher has a programmed approach to the concepts, skills, and attitudes she is teaching. That is, through learning tasks she teaches one introductory skill and concept. As learners use it, they find it applicable to their daily life and try it at home. They come back to class excited and motivated to learn the next complex concept or skill. This teacher is conscious of the principle of immediacy: the need of adult learners to be able to use what they are learning.

In a program on substance abuse in a community setting, the learners tell their stories of the destructiveness of their addictive habit. They do not urge their colleagues to abstain, but the immediacy of their story moves all who hear it. It is as though the listeners live vicariously the pain and fear of the storyteller. There is powerful immediacy in such programs.

Retraining men and women for new skills demands this principle, too. Unless adults see that their efforts are having practical and immediate results, they rarely continue a retraining program. Designing and leading such a skill-based program in a setting where jobs requiring the new skill are available is a cogent application of the principle of immediacy.

New Roles for Dialogue

Every adult educator who has tried to use the dialogue approach has stories to tell about the difficulty caused when learners see a confusion of roles. "Tell us what you want us to know!" learners implore. They are initially confused about who is the decision maker about what is to be taught. Why are you asking them their expectations? Why are they asked to talk to other students in the class? Who has a deliberative voice? Who can offer suggestions about the content of a course, the processes being used, or the time arrangements? Why are you offering them this consultative voice? I find it best to address these questions through the learning tasks, rather than using monologue to lecture on the virtues of dialogue. However, the initial resistance of adult learners who are used to a more passive role is not surprising.

Teaching adults to use new farm machinery that will increase the productivity of their land is a common agricultural extension effort. The role of the extension agent is manifold: technician, adviser, resource person, coach, evaluator. Some of these roles may be shared by learners as they work in small groups or teams. Some of these roles will change as the learners become more proficient in the skill. In a dialogue education setting, the agent will herself take a learning role as she listens to the questions and suggestions of the farmers. What this principle stresses is that the roles must be clear and ambiguity must be avoided. If farmers see the agent as the decision maker about what type of new machines they should purchase for their farms—and that is not the agent's role at all—this point needs to be clarified.

In teaching teachers to use the principles and practices of dialogue education, our staff often speak of themselves as future resources. Students can call at any time to review a program or locate a missing reference. However, if students see staff as those who will design their programs for them, they need to be told very clearly that they are wrong. Clarity of role is the issue here.

Teamwork

Teamwork is as much a practice as a principle of dialogue education. Many of the stories in this book refer to teamwork and work in small groups. I have defined a learning task as an open question put to a small group with the resources they need to respond to it (Vella, 2000). Even when working with a large group of adults, we can use small subgroups and teams to do certain learning tasks. In training men and women for a particular trade, practice in skills can be accomplished in small groups for reinforcement, feedback, and efficient learning. I have "taught" audiences of over a thousand people, asking them to turn to their neighbors, form small groups for themselves, and do a learning task. The energy released when men and women do such a task is surprising. When you invite a "chorus of conversations" in lieu of your monologue, when you invite learners to find their own voice and not listen only to yours, you invite a quantum leap into learning.

In teaching adults how to invest their resources, purchase a home, or select a useful and durable vehicle, we can invite them to work together on learning tasks and watch the peer education, group bonding, and learning that occur. Individual efforts at learning are sometimes necessary. But pitting individuals against one another in a destructive competition is alien to dialogue education. We live and learn together.

Engagement

Without engagement there is no learning. We know this from our own learning experience. The protocols of formal learning, however, put the burden of engagement on the learners. Their response to a formal lecture is entirely up to them. In dialogue education we design programs based on a competent learning needs and resources assessment that is engaging. If we accept that we can set learning tasks as open questions put to a small group with the materials and resources they need to respond, we know how to engage learners. All the successful educational programs you have designed, taught, and celebrated in your life were those in which learners were deeply engaged.

Efforts to "cover" a set curriculum often lead to neglect of this principle of engagement. Our job in adult education is not to cover a set of course materials, but to engage adults in effective and significant learning. As community banks educate more families about alternatives to funding the purchase of a home or a vehicle or the kinds of investments they can make, the engagement of these men and women in this learning as active subjects—decision makers—is vital. They have important questions to ask about their land, their rights, and their responsibilities as they face the first mortgage of their lives. Bankers, in turn, have much to learn from such an engaging dialogue with these clients.

Accountability

How do they know they know? This is the accountability question that reaches back to touch all the other principles and practices. Each of the stories in this book portrays our efforts to make the educational event accountable to the learners.

We may suddenly stop in the midst of a workshop and say: "Wait! I can see that many of you are having trouble with this complex concept. Let's form small groups to work it through once more with feeling." You name group leaders from among those who apparently comprehend the concept and say: "You five each get a small group around you to work on this learning task, and let me know what I can do to help. We are not leaving this item until I'm convinced that you all know that you know it!" Can you imagine the effect that will have on test scores?

The portfolio of products resulting from learning tasks will show you and each learner that the achievement based objectives have been completed and the named content learned. Consider what might be in such a portfolio for a course you are teaching to welfare mothers on the resources afforded them under a new law, a workshop for managers on diversity in the workplace, or a seminar for adult educators on quantum thinking.

Dialogue education is as accountable as the design of it.

Honest Dialogue

Paulo Freire describes how in a dialogue approach to adult learning the teacher learns and the learner teaches. I trust this was obvious in all the stories told here. I learned at least as much as any of the participants in any of those learning events.

A story from my Tanzanian experience might make the value of dialogue clear. We were teaching a group of church teachers at a distant parish. My colleague had gone into town for supplies, and I was leading the session on a hot afternoon. The men, all in their thirties and forties, got into a jolly mood. They began acting quite frivolous, laughing and telling jokes during the learning tasks. I lost my temper and in an uncharacteristic outburst said to these adults: "Please, you've got to get serious about this work! This workshop has cost a lot of money! We've got to get down to business."

I knew from the silence that filled that room that I had stepped outside all bounds of propriety. At least I had the good grace to keep still as Tomas got up to say to his fellows, "I am going to get the afternoon bus home! What Jane has said has cut me to the heart." One by one the men got up and each had a word to say to me. They were polite and clear. One said, "I may look poor, but when you come to my village you will see houses that I have built, and a farm that I plow, and a family of many children. That is my wealth!"

At one point during their declamations, my colleague arrived on the scene. I motioned to her to sit down. She listened to the men and wondered what in the world had happened. I did have the good grace to sit still, keep quiet, and pay attention. When they finished, they were standing, ready to leave. I said, in a choked voice, "Gentlemen, I have been teaching in Tanzania for almost twenty years. No one has ever spoken to me with this kind of honesty before. I had no idea of the significance of what I said. I apologize sincerely and I thank you for your honesty."

The group of adult men looked at one another, smiled at the two of us, and sat down. They moved back to the task at hand very naturally until they were interrupted by Tomas, who looked up from his work to announce, "I just want to say I am not taking that two o'clock bus home!"

When adult students ask me about the best learning experience in my life, I usually tell that story. I see that the quantum concepts we have examined in this book were working there for me. The importance of relationship, energy, participation, uncertainty, duality, and wholeness were implicit in my silence and my learning.

Julius Nyerere, the late philosopher-president of Tanzania, said that he wanted the nation to grow out of its own roots. This is true not only for nations but also for individuals. As we continue to search for principles and practices of adult learning—of dialogue education—that might apply in diverse situations, we educators must celebrate our own ability to listen, learn, and grow out of our own roots.

17

How Do You Know You Know?

Supposing and Proposing

We know that merely reading a book does not change behavior. But let us suppose that you have not read this book. You have never met Fatuma, Jean Pierre, the doctors of the International Center for the Control of Diarrheal Disease, or Durga. You have never heard of the seven steps of design, the principles of dialogue education, or the six quantum concepts.

Supposing

You have the occasion to plan a course for adult learners. What do you do? You probably consider what it is you want to teach them, organize that content into reasonable and cogent units, and give it to them one way or another. You may use a video or a lecture or invite small-group discussions. You will probably not be aware that some of your questions are closed or that the sequence in your presentation is inappropriate. You may not recognize the need for reinforcement. You may struggle valiantly with the distance that separates you culturally, cognitively, by age, or by gender from the learners. You may not be aware that you are not using their generative themes and, therefore, your well-prepared content can be lost on them. You probably did not do a learning needs and resources assessment or ask the learners their expectations of the course. Since you did not use the seven steps of design, you have not been intentional about the time frame or the site of the course.

You probably do not know you need to work toward optimal dialogue about the content with the learners as subjects or decision makers. You probably teach very well without recognizing that your teaching does not ensure their learning. There are probably no learning tasks in your outline. It is likely that a lot of the work you do involves cognitive content without attention to the affective and psychomotor aspects. At the end of the course, you may use an evaluation instrument that measures their cognitive learning. You will probably not ask yourself: How do they know they know?

You probably are not aware of the importance of relationship, the use of energy, the honoring of duality and uncertainty, and the fact that learners' perception and participation are operative.

Reading this book, therefore, could make a difference in your preparation, your teaching, and the means you choose to evaluate their learning.

The mother of a dear friend recently described her first venture into the world of computers. She decided to take a continuing education course at a community college. She paid her tuition, purchased her textbook, and bravely entered the first class. She was surrounded by other white-haired grandmothers. They, too, had finally recognized that they must breach the wall separating them from computer literacy. The young, enthusiastic teacher spent the first class preaching in a language my friend's mother could not understand: bits, bytes, RAM, CD-ROM! She waited for the moment when they would learn how to turn the computer on. It never came. After fifty minutes of listening to well-organized but incomprehensible teaching, she and many of her peers ran from the class, never to return. The world of computers is still a fearful unknown to these courageous seniors. But suppose that young teacher had read this book. What difference might that have made for those women?

Proposing

You have read this book. The seven steps of design are yours to use as you begin to design your course, training, orientation, or workshop. Your efforts at dialogue through learning needs and resources analysis, open questions, learning tasks, and evaluation invite adult learners to participate and examine the content you are teaching. As subjects of the learning, they argue and share their different values and perceptions with you in an exciting learning dialogue. Your learning tasks are cognitive, affective, and psychomotor. People are using all their senses, their potential for affect, and their muscles as they learn. They are doing it. The immediacy of their learning motivates them to further examination and praxis. The quantum concepts are at play as you respect the relatedness of all that you teach, honor inevitable duality, embrace uncertainty, and work toward unleashing the energy of the learners. You work from a holistic perspective and recognize that each learner brings a unique perspective from his or her context.

Because you are using small groups, these adults are sharing their lives and value systems with one another, focused by the content they are learning together. They are, in fact, teaching one another. There is stimulating competition going on. The materials they are using reflect their own language and their own themes, which you heard during the learning needs and resources assessment. Since your questions are mostly open, they recognize that your role is not only expert in the content area but also learner. The safety in the course invites some surprising questions from the adult learners—taking you all to levels of learning you may not have anticipated. As you listen and learn together, you and they can celebrate the power of dialogue.

Appendix:
Ways to Do Needs Assessment

Here are some specific ways to do a learning needs and resources assessment.

Shared Survey

By e-mail, ask a set of three or four questions after sending the *who*, *why*, *when*, *where*, *what*, and *what for* of the seven design steps to those registered for your course. Tell them you will forward their response to their classmates. This way, everyone gets to know what all participants are hoping for from the course. You begin, not only the dialogue, but also the community building.

Here are the short questions we used recently for a five-day course at the Peace Institute of Eastern Mennonite University:

1. Describe your involvement in Peace Education.
2. You have read the syllabus for the course. Name, in the light of that syllabus, your hopes for the week. That is, what do you hope to learn and accomplish by the end of the week?
3. Describe a recent situation where you designed or taught a session related to peace education.

My colleague and I studied the responses to these questions and discovered a set of common needs that we saw we could meet by a simple adjustment to the program.

Designs

Invite participants to send to you the lesson plan of a course they have recently taught. This gives you a good sense of how learners think about design. It is helpful then to return this initial design to them at the end of the course. They can compare it to the designs they have just completed in the course and see how far they have moved and how much they have learned.

Video

A videotape of the participant teaching is excellent baseline material for a course on dialogue education. Again, this video can be compared by them at the end of the course to the videotapes of their teaching during the course. You do not have to view the entire needs assessment video to get a sense of what they need to learn. Viewing a small clip will do.

Learning Biography

Invite learners to reflect on how they have learned in their lives. Ask: When was the best learning experience? When did you learn something that moved you in a new direction? When did you feel uncomfortable in a learning situation?

This will give you a picture of their experience as learners and begin their reflection on how people learn. An adaptation of this for a course on gardening, of course, would be inviting reflection on the gardens they have developed over the years. Or for a course on cooking, invite them to share their own favorite recipes or some they have developed. As you see, needs assessment is also a study of the resources the participants bring to a learning event.

Identification of Issues

Invite participants in a course to describe one issue they have with the content they are learning. For example, if you are teaching investment strategies, invite learners to describe when they invested and lost their money; ask them to identify the resources they have used that they find confusing or intimidating.

As learners name their own issues and problems with the content, they are motivating themselves to work toward not only solving those problems but also preventing their occurring again.

Vision Building

Invite learners in a class or a course to describe what their lives will look like when they have the skills and knowledge this course offers.

Can you show learners how you, as designer and teacher, are engaging them at the outset in the results of the course?

Interviews

It is always a joy to talk to participants prior to a course or workshop, either by phone or in person, if that is possible. If you are working with the teaching staff at a school, for example, talk not only to the teachers but also to the secretarial staff, the administrators, and a sample of parents. To get such a diverse set of perspectives enriches the potential learning of the course.

An open-ended interview can be framed by a question: Please take a few minutes to tell me what you hope will be the results of this course on evaluation and accountability that I am leading with the teachers of this school. You will be surprised and delighted to discover how concerned and articulate the people you interview are. They will inevitably thank you for asking them!

From what we learned in Chapter Seven at McGee's Crossroads, we know that we need to speak not only to participants but also to others who are involved in the educational event. Here's what I could have done in McGee's Crossroads. I could have drawn a set of circles. Then, in the middle I could have written the names of the participants, in the next circle the names of the mayor of the town and the members of the town council, in the next circle the name of the grower and names of his staff, and so on. I hope you have learned from this story that we cannot ever deal with one part of the whole as though it stood alone. Everything is connected. That's good quantum thinking!

References

Adams, F. *Unearthing Seeds of Fire: The Idea of Highlander*. Mounteagle, Tenn.:
    John Blair, 1975.

Blackburn, S. *Think*. Oxford, U.K.: Oxford University Press, 2000.

Bloom, B. S. *Taxonomy of Educational Objectives*. New York: McKay, 1956.

Bryson, J. *Strategic Planning for Public and Nonprofit Organizations: A Guide to
    Strengthening and Sustaining Organizational Achievement*. San Francisco:
    Jossey-Bass, 1988.

Campbell, J. *Myths to Live By*. New York: Viking, 1972.

Campbell, J. *The Power of Myth*. New York: Doubleday, 1988.

Capra, F. *The Turning Point*. New York: Bantam, 1983

Cardenal, F., and Miller, V. "Nicaragua 1980: The Battle of the ABCs." *Harvard
    Educational Review*, 1981, *51*(1), 9–29.

Eliot, T. S. "Tradition and the Individual Talent." In F. Kermode (ed.), *Selected
    Prose of T. S. Eliot*. New York: Harcourt, 1975.

Freire, P. *Cultural Action for Freedom*. Monograph Series, no. 1. Cambridge,
    Mass.: Harvard Educational Review, 1970.

Freire, P. *Pedagogy of the Oppressed*. New York: Herder and Herder, 1972.

Freire, P., and Faundez, A. *Learning to Question: A Pedagogy of Liberation*. New
    York: Herder and Herder, 1972.

Freire, P., and Horton, M. *We Make the Road by Walking: Conversations on Educa-
    tion and Social Change*. Philadelphia: Temple University Press, 1990.

Gravett, Sarah. *Adult Learning*. Pretoria, South Africa: Van Schaik Publishers, 2001.

Hutchinson, T. "Community Needs Analysis Methodology" (unpublished
    paper). University of Massachusetts, 1978.

Johnson, D., and Johnson, F. *Joining Together: Group Theory and Group Skills*.
    Englewood Cliffs, N.J.: Prentice-Hall, 1991.

Jung, C. *The Collected Works*. Princeton: Princeton University Press, 1969.

Kingsolver, B. *The Poisonwood Bible*. New York: HarperCollins, 1999.

Knowles, M. *The Modern Practice of Adult Education: An Autobiographical Journey*. New York: Association Press, 1970.

Knox, A. *Helping Adults Learn: A Guide to Planning, Implementing, and Conducting Programs*. San Francisco: Jossey-Bass, 1986.

Kuhn, T. *The Structure of Scientific Revolutions*. Chicago: University of Chicago Press, 1970.

Lazear, D. *Seven Ways of Knowing: Teaching for Multiple Intelligence*. Palatine, Ill.: Skylight Publishing, 1991.

Oliver, D., with Waldron Gershman, K. *Education, Modernity and Fractured Meaning*. Albany, N.Y.: SUNY Press, 1989.

Srinivasan, L. *Options for Educators*. New York: Private Agencies Cooperating Together/Community Development Service, 1992.

STAR POWER: A Simulation. Del Mar, Calif.: Simulation Training Systems, 1993

Vella, J. *Community Education for Self-Reliant Development*. (Unpublished dissertation) Amherst: Center for International Development, University of Massachusetts, 1978.

Vella, J. *Learning to Teach*. New York: Women, Ink, 1989.

Vella, J *Training Through Dialogue*. San Francisco: Jossey-Bass, 1995.

Vella, J. *Taking Learning to Task*. San Francisco: Jossey-Bass, 2000.

Vella, J., Berardinelli, P., and Burrow, J. *How Do They Know They Know?* San Francisco: Jossey-Bass, 1998.

Wink, W. *Engaging the Powers*. Minneapolis, Minn.: Fortress Press, 1992.

Wheatley, M. *Leadership and the New Science*. San Francisco: Berrett-Koehler, 1999.

Zohar, D. *Rewiring the Corporate Brain*. San Francisco: Berrett-Koehler, 1997.

Zohar, D., and Marshall, I. *The Quantum Self: Human Nature and Consciousness Defined by the New Physics*. New York: William Morrow, 1990.

Zohar, D., and Marshall, I. *Who's Afraid of Schrödinger's Cat?* New York: William Morrow, 1997.

Resources for Further Learning

Beamish, J., and Vella, J. *The Journalists' Guide*. Research Triangle Park, N.C.: Family Health International, 1997.

Bohm, D., and Peat, F. D. *Science, Order, and Creativity*. New York: Bantam, 1987.

Brookfield, S. *Adult Learners, Adult Education, and the Community*. New York: Teachers College Press, 1984.

Brookfield, S. *Understanding and Facilitating Adult Learning: A Comprehensive Analysis of Principles and Effective Practices*. San Francisco: Jossey-Bass, 1986.

Brookfield, S. *Developing Critical Thinkers: Challenging Adults to Explore Alternative Ways of Thinking and Acting*. San Francisco: Jossey-Bass, 1987.

Brookfield, S. *The Skillful Teacher: On Technique, Trust, and Responsiveness in the Classroom*. San Francisco: Jossey-Bass, 1990.

Capra, F. *The Turning Point*. New York: Bantam, 1983.

Einstein, A. *The Theory of Relativity*. New York: IMF Publications, 1950.

Freire, P. *The Politics of Education*. South Hadley, Mass.: Bergin & Garvey, 1985.

Freire, P., and Macedo, D. *Literacy: Reading the Word and the World*. New York: Bergin & Garvey, 1987.

Freire, P., and Shor, I. *A Pedagogy for Liberation: Dialogues on Transforming Education*. New York: Bergin & Garvey, 1987.

Hope, A., Timmel, S., and Hodzi, C. *Training for Transformation: A Handbook for Community Workers*. Harare, Zimbabwe: Mambo Press, 1984.

Hutchinson, T. "Community Needs Analysis Methodology." Unpublished paper. University of Massachusetts.

Gribben, J. *Schrodinger's Kittens and the Search for Reality: Solving the Quantum Mysteries*. Boston: Little Brown, 1995.

Kindervatter, S. *Nonformal Education as an Empowering Process*. Amherst: Center for International Education, University of Massachusetts, 1979.

Knowles, M. *The Modern Practice of Adult Education: An Autobiographical Journey*. New York: Association Press, 1970.

Knowles, M. *Self-Directed Learning: A Guide for Learners and Teachers*. Chicago: Follett, 1975.

Knowles, M. *The Adult Learner: A Neglected Species*. Houston: Gulf, 1978.

Knox, A. *Developing, Administering, and Evaluating Adult Education*. San Francisco: Jossey-Bass, 1980.

Knox, A. *Helping Adults Learn: A Guide to Planning, Implementing, and Conducting Programs*. San Francisco: Jossey-Bass, 1986.

Knowles, M. *The Making of an Adult Educator*. San Francisco: Jossey-Bass, 1989.

Lewin, K. *Field Theory in Social Science*. New York: HarperCollins, 1951.

Marshall, I., and Zohar, D. *Who's Afraid of Schrodinger's Cat?* New York: Quill Morrow, 1997.

Maturana, H., and Varela, F. *The Tree of Knowledge*. Boston: Shambhala, 1992.

Medsker, K., and Holdsworth, K. *Models and Strategies for Training Design*. Silver Spring, Md.: International Society for Performance Appraisal, 2001.

Memmi, A. *The Colonizer and the Colonized*. Boston: Beacon Press, 1965.

Mezirow, J. *Learning as Transformation*. San Francisco: Jossey-Bass, 2000.

Oliver, D. *Education and Community*. Berkeley, Calif.: McCutchan, 1976.

O'Murchu, D. *Quantum Theology*. New York: Crossroad, 2000.

Schön, D. *Educating the Reflective Practitioner: Toward a New Design for Teaching and Learning in the Professions*. San Francisco: Jossey-Bass, 1987.

Shor, I. *Critical Teaching and Everyday Life*. Montreal: Black Rose Books, 1980.

Srinivasan, L. *Perspectives on Nonformal Adult Learning*. New York: World Education, 1977.

Svendsen, D., and Wijetilleke, S. *Navamaga: Training Activities for Group Building, Health and Income Generation*. New York: Women, Ink, 1983.

Vella, J. *Learning to Teach*. New York: Women, Ink, 1989.

Vella, J. *Learning to Listen to Mothers*. Washington, D.C.: Academy for Educational Development, 1992.

Werner, D., and Bower, B. *Helping Health Workers Learn*. Palo Alto, Calif.: Hesperian Foundation, 1982.

Zohar, D., and Marshall, I. *The Quantum Self: Human Nature and Consciousness Defined by the New Physics*. New York: William Morrow, 1990.

Zohar, D. *Rewiring the Corporate Brain*. San Francisco: Berrett-Kohler, 1997.

Index

Immediacy principle: application of, 235–236; conducting effective meetings and, 40; immediate response to questions as, 97–98; implemented in El Salvador, 166, 167; overview of, 19–20; quantum concepts and, 34
Indonesian Save the Children training, 86
Inductive learning, 14

J

Johnson, D., 18, 150
Johnson, F., 18, 150
Jubilee Education Center: achievement based objectives of, 208; adult learners at, 204–205; design challenges of, 210–211; engagement facilitated by, 205–210; evaluation of, 209–210; program and process at, 205–209; situation at, 203–204
Jubilee Fellowship program: affirmation encouraged at, 90–91; design challenges of, 99–100; engagement in significant work used in, 96; evaluation phase of, 99; learning moments experienced at, 98–99; mutual mentoring at, 90; use of mutual respect at, 91–94; nonjudgmental dialogue used at, 94; process of, 87–98; relationships formed at, 88–89; use of time in, 89–90
Jubilee Popular Education Center (North Carolina), 86
Jung, C., 8, 92, 215

K

Keats, J., 93
Kingsolver, B., 105
"Knowing Oppression and Searching Our Resources for Liberation" module (Maryknoll workshop), 186
Knowledge (technical vs. ontological), 82, 150
Knowles, M., 3, 50, 173
Kuhn, T., 26, 97

"Kusikilizana" (to hear one another), 79

L

Learner decision making. See Respecting learners principle
Learning moment, 98–99
Learning tasks: accomplished by teams, 200–201; conducting meeting workshop on, 41–43; dialogue approach and, 185; as engagement in significant work, 96; during Ethiopian project, 65, 67; feedback as, 47; Maryknoll workshop, 183, 184, 185; NS (National Service) training course, 49–51; open dialogue, 92–93; used in sample two-hour workshop, 44–45; Zambian simulation, 156–158. See also Adult learners; Adult learning
Learning to Teach (Vella), 219
LeBan, K., 116, 122, 123
Lewin, K., 18, 96, 116, 150, 154, 235
Listening, using quantum theory for, 7–8
Listening/thematic analysis, 6–7
LNRA (learning needs and resources assessment): achieving meeting objectives using, 49; described, 57
Lori, Assura, 214, 215, 216, 217, 219

M

McGee's Crossroads, 109–110, 111
McLoughlin, J., 192
Madama Butterfly (Puccini, opera), 12
Makame, 73–74, 75, 77, 80
Makoko Family Center (Musoma): CED extension of, 73–74; CED program/process in, 74–77; design challenges and, 83; listening to community themes experience, 78–81; six considerations of CED program in, 77–78
Maldives community development training: design challenges of, 126–127; evaluation of, 125–126;

Teachers: advantage of engaged learners to, 211; clear communication roles of learner and, 20–22; consultative vs. deliberative voices of, 16; immediate response to questions by, 97–98; learning tasks role by, 42–43; listening effort by, 6; power relationship between learners and, 86–87; *Pray for doubt!* motto and, 165; respecting learner decision making, 15–17; safety principle guiding, 8–10; using sequence/reinforcement techniques, 12–14; sound relationship between learner and, 10–12

Teams: dialogue approach to build, 200, 237–238; Ethiopian project use of, 66–67, 68–69; hospice, 209; learning task accomplished by, 200–201; Zimbabwe literacy campaign, 194–196, 199–200

Teamwork principles: application of, 237–238; Ethiopian project use of, 66–67, 68–69; overview of, 22–24; quantum concepts and, 34; Zimbabwe literacy campaign use of, 191–201

Technical knowledge, 82, 150

Thematic analysis, 6–7

Think (Blackburn), 77

Tradition and the Individual Talent (Eliot), 110

Training Through Dialogue (Vella), 3

U

Ujamaa (familyhood), 80

Uncertainty: defining, 31; of education, 31–32; Jubilee Center use of engagement and, 211; Zambian story use of, 160

UNDP (United Nations Development Program), 117

University in Dacca, 214

University of North Carolina School of Public Health, 89, 93, 229

University of Zimbabwe, 198

Utheem Island, 116, 119

V

Vella, J., 14, 18, 21, 24, 37, 41, 47, 78, 86, 92, 97, 110, 142, 172, 184, 187, 199, 237

Volunteers in Service Overseas, 117

W

The Whaler (dinghy), 123–124

Wheatley, M., 6, 29, 85, 88, 104–105, 106–107, 158, 161

Wijeratne, E. E., 117

Wink, W., 91

Women: child saved by Musoma, 81; low status of Musoma, 79–80, 82

WWW question: Ethiopian aid project use of, 57, 64–65; overview of, 5, 8

Z

Zambian Episcopal Conference, 151

Zambian leadership training: adult learners of, 152; affective and psychomotor elements used in, 153–158; background and setting of, 150–152; design challenges of, 159–160; program and process of, 153–158; reflections on, 158–159; simulations used during, 153–158

Zimbabwe literacy campaign: adult learners of, 193–194; design challenges of, 200–201; evaluation of, 199–200; pedagogy of shared responsibility during, 196; political divisions determining two trainings of, 194–915; program and process of, 197–199; situation and setting of, 191–192; teams formed for, 194–196, 199–200

Zimbabwe Ministry of Education, 192, 193, 200

Zohar, D., 3, 4, 10, 15, 18, 21–22, 23, 25, 26, 29, 95, 185, 209, 232